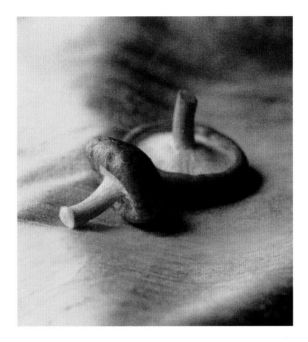

WILLIAMS-SONOMA

RISOTTO

RECIPES AND TEXT
PAMELA SHELDON JOHNS

GENERAL EDITOR
CHUCK WILLIAMS

PHOTOGRAPHS
NOEL BARNHURST

SIMON & SCHUSTER • SOURCE

NEW YORK • LONDON • TORONTO • SYDNEY • SINGAPORE

CONTENTS

POULTRY AND MEAT RISOTTOS

SPECIAL RISOTTO DISHES

DESSERT RISOTTOS

INTRODUCTION

Creamy, tender risotto is such a far cry from steamed rice that it is hard to believe they are made from the same basic ingredient. But it is important to know the rice used for risotto is a particular variety, rich in starch, which is slowly and carefully cooked in such a way that the rice releases its starch resulting in a creamy consistency while the grains of rice remain whole. Since risotto is such a simple dish, always use the best ingredients you can find: high-quality rice, fresh seasonal vegetables, good wine, flavorful stock, and sweet butter. Plus keep in mind that making risotto requires attention—from coating the rice with oil to stirring in stock just a ladleful at a time to adding the final seasonings.

If you turn to the informative basics section at the back of this book, you'll find everything you need to know to start making risotto at home. Choose any of the recipes in these pages, and once you taste the delicious results, you will find risotto is well worth the time and care it takes to prepare.

Chuck Williams

THE CLASSICS

The recipes in this chapter have evolved from a local ingredient, such as the seafood of the Veneto or the white truffle of Piedmont. Or, they may feature an iconic seasonal ingredient, such as the asparagus of spring or the mushrooms of autumn. And, a simple unadorned risotto could be considered the most classic dish of all.

BASIC RISOTTO

In a saucepan over medium heat, bring the stock to a gentle simmer and maintain over low heat.

In a large, heavy saucepan, heat the oil over medium heat. Add the onion and sauté until softened, about 4 minutes. Add the rice and stir until each grain is well coated with oil and translucent with a white dot in the center, about 3 minutes. Add the wine and stir until it is completely absorbed.

Add the simmering stock a ladleful at a time, stirring frequently after each addition. Wait until the stock is almost completely absorbed (but the rice is never dry on top) before adding the next ladleful. Reserve ¼ cup (2 fl oz/60 ml) stock to add at the end.

When the rice is almost tender to the bite but slightly firm in the center and looks creamy, after about 20 minutes, remove from the heat and stir in butter to taste and the reserved ¼ cup stock. Season to taste with salt and pepper and serve at once.

MAKES 6 SERVINGS

6 cups (48 fl oz/1.5 l) chicken stock (page 110)

¼ cup (2 fl oz/60 ml) extra-virgin olive oil

½ cup (2½ oz/75 g) finely chopped yellow onion

2 cups (14 oz/440 g) Arborio or Carnaroli rice

1 cup (8 fl oz/250 ml) dry white wine, at room temperature

1–2 tablespoons unsalted butter

Salt and freshly ground pepper

BUTTER

In Italy, a simple, plain risotto is often served as a first course or side dish to complement a main-course meat dish. This basic risotto recipe adds nothing but butter as a flavoring—so the butter should be the best you can find. Use unsalted butter, which is apt to be fresher than salted and also allows you to better control the seasoning of the dish. Seek out European-style butter such as Keller's, which contains less moisture and more flavorful butterfat.

RISOTTO WITH ASPARAGUS

1 lb (500 g) asparagus, trimmed and cut into 2-inch (5-cm) lengths

7–8 cups (56–64 fl oz/ 1.75–2 l) chicken stock (page 110)

¼ cup (2 fl oz/60 ml) extra-virgin olive oil

½ cup (2½ oz/75 g) finely chopped yellow onion

3 cups (21 oz/655 g) Arborio or Carnaroli rice

1 cup (8 fl oz/250 ml) dry white wine, at room temperature

1 tablespoon unsalted butter

¼ cup (1 oz/30 g) freshly grated Parmesan cheese

Salt and freshly ground pepper

Parboil the asparagus in salted boiling water until just tender, 1–2 minutes *(right)*. Set aside.

In a saucepan over medium heat, bring the stock to a gentle simmer and maintain over low heat.

In a large, heavy saucepan, heat the oil over medium heat. Add the onion and sauté until softened, about 4 minutes. Add the rice and stir until each grain is well coated with oil and translucent with a white dot in the center, about 3 minutes. Add the wine and stir until it is completely absorbed.

Add the simmering stock a ladleful at a time, stirring frequently after each addition. Wait until the stock is almost completely absorbed (but the rice is never dry on top) before adding the next ladleful. Reserve ¼ cup (2 fl oz/60 ml) stock to add at the end.

When the rice is almost tender to the bite but slightly firm in the center and looks creamy, after about 18 minutes, add the asparagus and a ladleful of stock. Cook, stirring occasionally, until the the asparagus is heated through and the rice is al dente, 2–3 minutes longer. Remove from the heat and stir in the butter, cheese, and reserved ¼ cup stock. Season to taste with salt and pepper and serve at once.

MAKES 6 SERVINGS

PARBOILING VEGETABLES

Parboiling vegetables sets their color and partially cooks them. To parboil, plunge the vegetable in a large quantity of salted boiling water and cook until the vegetable brightens in color and just begins to soften. Drain and plunge immediately into a large bowl of ice water to stop the cooking. Let cool for about 30 seconds, drain again, and set aside until ready to use. The parboiling time depends on the density of the vegetable. For example, slender asparagus will take 1–2 minutes, while thick carrots will take 3–4 minutes.

RISOTTO WITH MUSHROOMS

In a saucepan, bring the stock to a simmer. Remove from the heat and add the dried porcini. Soak for 20 minutes. Drain the mushrooms through a sieve lined with a double layer of cheesecloth (muslin), gently pressing against the mushrooms to force out the stock and reserving the stock. Return the stock to the saucepan and bring to a simmer over medium heat. Maintain at a gentle simmer over low heat. Chop the porcini and set aside.

In a large, heavy saucepan, heat the olive oil over medium heat. Add the garlic and sauté until softened, about 2 minutes. Add all the fresh mushrooms and cook until softened, about 5 minutes. Add the chopped porcini, parsley, thyme, and ½ cup (4 fl oz/125 ml) of the simmering stock and cook until thickened, about 5 minutes. Using a slotted spoon, transfer the mushrooms to a bowl and set aside.

Add the rice to the same pan and stir over medium heat until each grain is translucent with a white dot in the center, about 3 minutes. Add the wine and stir until it is completely absorbed.

Add the simmering stock a ladleful at a time, stirring frequently after each addition. Wait until the stock is almost completely absorbed (but the rice is never dry on top) before adding the next ladleful. Reserve ¼ cup (2 fl oz/60 ml) stock to add at the end.

When the rice is almost tender to the bite but slightly firm in the center and looks creamy, after about 18 minutes, add the mushroom mixture and a ladleful of stock. Cook, stirring occasionally, until the mushrooms are heated through and the rice is al dente, 2–3 minutes longer. Remove from the heat and stir in the butter and reserved ¼ cup stock. Season to taste with salt and pepper and serve at once.

MAKES 6 SERVINGS

PORCINO MUSHROOMS

If you are in Italy in autumn, you are likely to see cars pulled off the road, their passengers roaming wooded areas with baskets on their arms, in search of one of the season's delicacies: porcino mushrooms (ceps). Even when they are in season, fresh porcini may be difficult to find outside of Italy, so try other flavorful wild mushrooms, such as shiitakes or chanterelles. Dried porcini, widely available, are packed with flavor, and only a small amount is needed to impart their evocative woodsy essence.

8–9 cups (64–72 fl oz/2–2.1 l) chicken stock (page 110)

½ oz (15 g) dried porcino mushrooms (ceps)

¼ cup (2 fl oz/60 ml) extra-virgin olive oil

4 cloves garlic, minced

½ lb (250 g) assorted fresh wild mushrooms such as shiitake, portobello, oyster, and chanterelle, brushed clean and thinly sliced

½ lb (250 g) fresh white cultivated mushrooms, brushed clean and thinly sliced

¼ cup (⅓ oz/10 g) minced fresh flat-leaf (Italian) parsley

2 teaspoons minced fresh thyme

3 cups (21 oz/655 g) Arborio or Carnaroli rice

1 cup (8 fl oz/250 ml) dry white wine, at room temperature

2 tablespoons unsalted butter

Salt and freshly ground pepper

RISOTTO WITH GRILLED SHELLFISH

Juice of 1 lemon

¼ cup (2 fl oz/60 ml) plus 3 tablespoons extra-virgin olive oil

Salt and freshly ground pepper

¾ lb (375 g) shrimp (prawns), peeled and deveined (page 115)

¾ lb (375 g) sea scallops

1 small red onion, cut into 1-inch (2.5-cm) pieces

7–8 cups (56–64 fl oz/ 1.75–2 l) shellfish stock (page 111) or chicken stock (page 110)

¼ cup (1 oz/30 g) finely chopped green (spring) onion, including tender green tops, plus finely chopped green tops for garnish

3 cups (21 oz/655 g) Arborio or Carnaroli rice

1 cup (8 fl oz/250 ml) dry white wine, at room temperature

2 tablespoons unsalted butter

12 wooden skewers, soaked in water for 30 minutes, or metal skewers

In a small bowl, whisk together the lemon juice and the 3 tablespoons oil. Season to taste with salt and pepper. Drain the skewers and thread them alternately with the shrimp, scallops, and red onion pieces, dividing them evenly. Coat lightly with the lemon-oil mixture. Set aside.

Prepare a fire in a charcoal grill.

In a saucepan over medium heat, bring the stock to a gentle simmer and maintain over low heat.

In a large, heavy saucepan, heat the ¼ cup oil over medium heat. Add the green onion and sauté until softened, 2–3 minutes. Add the rice and stir until each grain is well coated with oil and translucent with a white dot in the center, about 3 minutes. Add the wine and stir until it is completely absorbed.

Add the simmering stock a ladleful at a time, stirring frequently after each addition. Wait until the stock is almost completely absorbed (but the rice is never dry on top) before adding the next ladleful. Reserve ¼ cup (2 fl oz/60 ml) stock to add at the end.

When the rice is almost tender to the bite but slightly firm in the center and looks creamy, after about 18 minutes, grill the skewers, turning once, until the shellfish are firm and opaque, about 1 minute on each side. When the rice is al dente, after 2–3 minutes longer, remove from the heat and stir in the butter and the reserved ¼ cup stock. Season to taste with salt and pepper. Transfer to a warmed platter. Remove the shellfish and onions from the skewers and arrange on top of the risotto. Alternatively, arrange the whole skewers on top of the risotto. Sprinkle with the green onion tops and serve at once.

MAKES 6 SERVINGS

GRILLING SAVVY

Grilling over hardwood charcoal imparts a wonderful aroma to shrimp and scallops. To keep the food from sticking, oil the grill and make sure it is hot before placing the skewers on it. Once the skewers are on the grill, don't move them for at least 30 seconds to prevent the meat from tearing. If you don't have a charcoal grill, lightly oil a broiler (grill) pan. Preheat the broiler and broil (grill) the skewers 4 inches (10 cm) from the heat source until the shellfish are firm and opaque throughout, 1–1½ minutes on each side.

RISOTTO WITH FOUR CHEESES

In a saucepan over medium heat, bring the stock to a gentle simmer and maintain over low heat.

In a large, heavy saucepan, heat the oil over medium heat. Add the onion and sauté until softened, about 4 minutes. Add the rice and stir until each grain is well coated with oil and translucent with a white dot in the center, about 3 minutes. Add the wine and stir until it is completely absorbed.

Add the simmering stock a ladleful at a time, stirring frequently after each addition. Wait until the stock is almost completely absorbed (but the rice is never dry on top) before adding the next ladleful. Reserve ¼ cup (2 fl oz/60 ml) stock to add at the end.

When the rice is tender to the bite but slightly firm in the center and looks creamy, after about 20 minutes, remove from the heat and stir in the reserved ¼ cup stock and the cheeses. Season to taste with salt and pepper, sprinkle with the parsley, and serve immediately.

MAKES 6 SERVINGS

ITALIAN CHEESES

Italy boasts more than four hundred regional cheeses. Of these, thirty have been defined by law as to place of origin and cheese-making process. These cheeses bear the designation "D.O.P.," or "protected designation of origin," to indicate compliance with the legal formula. D.O.P. cheeses are found all over Italy, and a popular pasta sauce called *quattro formaggi* (four cheeses) has evolved that uses a mixture of local favorites. Here, a blend of creamy young cheeses and harder aged cheeses adds mild yet complex flavor to this risotto.

7–8 cups (56–64 fl oz/ 1.75–2 l) chicken stock (page 110)

¼ cup (2 fl oz/60 ml) extra-virgin olive oil

½ cup (2½ oz/75 g) finely chopped yellow onion

3 cups (21 oz/655 g) Arborio or Carnaroli rice

1 cup (8 fl oz/250 ml) dry white wine, at room temperature

½ cup (3 oz/90 g) mascarpone cheese

⅓ cup (1½ oz/45 g) crumbled dolcelatte Gorgonzola cheese

¼ cup (1 oz/30 g) freshly grated Parmesan cheese

¼ cup (1 oz/30 g) grated Asiago cheese

Salt and freshly ground pepper

2 tablespoons minced fresh flat-leaf (Italian) parsley

RISI E BISI

7 cups (56 fl oz/1.75 l) chicken stock (page 110)

¼ cup (2 fl oz/60 ml) extra-virgin olive oil

1 yellow onion, finely chopped

1 carrot, peeled and finely diced

1 celery stalk, finely diced

6 oz (185 g) pancetta, coarsely chopped

1½ cups (10½ oz/330 g) Vialone Nano or Arborio rice

1 cup (8 fl oz/250 ml) dry white wine, at room temperature

2 teaspoons minced fresh flat-leaf (Italian) parsley

2 cups (10 oz/315 g) shelled fresh English peas

½ cup (2 oz/60 g) freshly grated Parmesan cheese

3 tablespoons unsalted butter

Salt and freshly ground pepper

In a saucepan over medium heat, bring the stock to a gentle simmer and maintain over low heat.

In a large, heavy saucepan, heat the olive oil over medium heat. Add the onion, carrot, and celery to the pan and sauté until the vegetables are softened, about 4 minutes. Add the pancetta and sauté until golden brown, about 5 minutes. Add the rice and stir until each grain is well coated with oil and translucent with a white dot in the center, about 3 minutes. Add the wine and stir until it is completely absorbed.

Add 2 cups (16 fl oz/500 ml) of the simmering stock, and the parsley. Reduce the heat to low. Continue to add the heated stock 1 cup (8 fl oz/250 ml) at a time, stirring frequently after each addition. Wait until the stock is almost completely absorbed (but the rice is never dry on top) before adding the next cupful. Reserve 1 cup stock to add at the end.

After 10 minutes, stir in the peas. When the rice and peas are tender, 8–10 minutes longer, stir in the reserved 1 cup stock. Remove from the heat and stir in the cheese and butter. Season to taste with salt and pepper and serve at once.

MAKES 4 SERVINGS

THE RETURN OF SPRING
This classic Venetian dish more closely resembles a soup than a traditional risotto. It is a looser, more liquidy risotto than most. The peas announce the arrival of spring, and the rice symbolizes the abundance to come with the return of warmer weather. In the past, this soup was offered to the duke of Venice on April 25, the feast day of St. Mark, patron saint of the city. The preferred rice for *risi e bisi* is Vialone Nano, a fine pearly grain cultivated primarily in the Veneto region.

RISOTTO WITH WHITE TRUFFLE

(page 110)

In a saucepan over medium heat, bring the stock to a gentle simmer and maintain over low heat.

In a large, heavy saucepan, heat the oil over medium heat. Add the onion and sauté until softened, about 4 minutes. Add the rice and stir until each grain is well coated with oil and translucent with a white dot in the center, about 3 minutes. Add the wine and stir until it is completely absorbed.

Add the simmering stock a ladleful at a time, stirring frequently after each addition. Wait until the stock is almost completely absorbed (but the rice is never dry on top) before adding the next ladleful. Reserve ¼ cup (2 fl oz/60 ml) stock to add at the end.

When the rice is tender to the bite but slightly firm in the center and looks creamy, after about 20 minutes, remove from the heat and stir in the butter and reserved ¼ cup stock. If using truffle oil, add it now. Season to taste with salt and pepper. If using the white truffle, season the risotto, divide it among warmed shallow bowls, and shave the truffle over each serving. Serve at once.

MAKES 6 SERVINGS

WHITE TRUFFLE OIL

White truffle oil is widely available, but its quality varies from brand to brand. Most truffle oils are flavored with a synthetic chemical compound that simulates the earthy aroma of truffles. For better flavor, look for an oil that lists truffle among its ingredients, preferably one with tiny bits of truffle in the bottle. For a special treat, seek out fresh white truffles for this dish (they are in season October through December). White truffles are never cooked. Just before serving, use a truffle slicer, mandoline, or vegetable peeler to shave a few truffle slices as thinly as possible over each bowl of risotto.

7–8 cups (56–64 fl oz/ 1.75–2 l) chicken stock (page 110)

¼ cup (2 fl oz/60 ml) extra-virgin olive oil

½ cup (2½ oz/75 g) finely chopped yellow onion

3 cups (21 oz/655 g) Arborio or Carnaroli rice

1 cup (8 fl oz/250 ml) dry white wine, at room temperature

2 tablespoons unsalted butter

1 teaspoon white truffle oil or ½ oz (15 g) white truffle

Salt and freshly ground pepper

SAFFRON RISOTTO WITH OSSO BUCO

¾ cup (4 oz/125 g)
all-purpose (plain) flour

Salt and ground pepper

6 veal shanks, cut into pieces
1½ inches (4 cm) thick

½ cup (4 fl oz/125 ml) olive oil

1 yellow onion, chopped

1 carrot, peeled and diced

1 celery stalk, diced

2 cloves garlic, minced

1½ cups (12 fl oz/375 ml) red
wine, at room temperature

5 cups (40 fl oz/1.25 l) meat
stock (page 110)

FOR THE SAFFRON RISOTTO:

7–8 cups (56–64 fl oz/1.75–
2 l) meat stock (page 110)

¼ cup (2 fl oz/60 ml) olive oil

½ cup (2½ oz/75 g) finely
chopped yellow onion

3 cups (21 oz/655 g) Arborio
or Carnaroli rice

1 cup (8 fl oz/250 ml) white
wine, at room temperature

2 pinches of saffron threads

4 tablespoons (2 oz/60 g)
unsalted butter

1 cup (4 oz/125 g) freshly
grated Parmesan cheese

Salt and ground pepper

Put the flour in a shallow dish and season with salt and pepper. Dredge the veal shank pieces, coating them evenly with the flour and shaking off the excess. Tie each with a piece of kitchen string to hold the meat to the bone. In a heavy frying pan, heat the oil over medium-high heat. Add the veal shanks and brown for about 4 minutes on each side. Transfer to a plate and set aside.

Reduce the heat to medium and add the onion, carrot, celery, and garlic. Sauté until softened, about 4 minutes. Add the wine and deglaze the pan, stirring to scrape up the browned bits from the bottom. Cook over high heat to reduce the liquid by half. Add the stock and reduce the heat to a simmer. Return the veal to the pan. Cover and cook, turning occasionally, for 1 hour. Remove the lid and cook until the shanks are tender, about 30 minutes longer.

About 30 minutes before the veal is done, make the risotto. In a saucepan over medium heat, bring the stock to a simmer and maintain over low heat. In a large, heavy saucepan over medium heat, heat the oil. Add the onion and sauté until softened, about 4 minutes. Add the rice and stir until each grain is well coated with oil and translucent with a white dot in the center, about 3 minutes. Add the wine and stir until completely absorbed.

Add the hot stock a ladleful at a time, stirring frequently after each addition. Wait until the stock is almost completely absorbed (but the rice is never dry on top) before adding the next ladleful. Reserve ¼ cup (2 fl oz/60 ml) stock and add the saffron to it.

When the rice is tender to the bite but slightly firm in the center and looks creamy, after about 20 minutes, add the saffron-infused stock. Remove from the heat and stir in the butter and cheese. Season to taste with salt and pepper. Transfer the risotto to a warmed platter. Top with the veal shanks and sprinkle with *gremolata (right)*, if using. Serve at once.

MAKES 6 SERVINGS

GREMOLATA

The classic way to serve this saffron risotto, known as *risotto milanese,* is topped with osso buco and garnished with *gremolata,* a piquant mixture of lemon, garlic, and parsley. To make *gremolata,* combine ½ cup (¾ oz/20 g) minced fresh flat-leaf (Italian) parsley, the grated zest of 1 lemon, and 2 minced cloves garlic. Set aside until ready to serve, then sprinkle over the top of the osso buco and risotto.

VEGETABLE RISOTTOS

Vegetable risottos reflect the seasons. Spring is welcomed with fava (broad) beans, artichokes, and spinach, while the warmth of summer is captured in a risotto made with tomatoes and basil. Autumn and winter risottos are comfort foods, especially when laced with radicchio, leeks, sun-dried tomatoes, roasted butternut squash, or beets.

RISOTTO WITH FAVA BEANS
28

RISOTTO WITH ARTICHOKES
31

RISOTTO WITH SPINACH
32

RISOTTO CAPRESE
35

RISOTTO WITH RADICCHIO
36

RISOTTO WITH ROASTED BUTTERNUT SQUASH
39

RISOTTO WITH LEEKS AND SUN-DRIED TOMATOES
40

RISOTTO WITH BEETS
43

RISOTTO WITH FAVA BEANS

In a saucepan over medium heat, bring the stock to a gentle simmer and maintain over low heat.

In a large, heavy saucepan, heat the oil over medium heat. Add the onion, carrot, and celery and sauté until golden brown, about 6 minutes. Add the rice and stir until each grain is well coated with oil and translucent with a white dot in the center, about 3 minutes. Add the wine and stir until it is completely absorbed.

Add the simmering stock a ladleful at a time, stirring frequently after each addition. Wait until the stock is almost completely absorbed (but the rice is never dry on top) before adding the next ladleful. Reserve ¼ cup (2 fl oz/60 ml) stock to add at the end.

When the rice is almost tender to the bite but slightly firm in the center and looks creamy, after about 18 minutes, add the fava beans and a ladleful of stock. Cook, stirring occasionally, until the fava beans are tender and heated through and the rice is al dente, 2–3 minutes longer. (Larger, more mature beans may need a little more time.) Remove from the heat and stir in the butter, cheese, and reserved ¼ cup stock. Season to taste with salt and pepper and serve at once.

MAKES 6 SERVINGS

FAVA BEANS

The appearance of fresh fava beans in the market signals the arrival of spring. Try to find them early in their short season. Favas, also called broad beans, must be shelled from their long green pods, then each bean must be blanched and skinned.

To blanch the shelled beans, plunge them into salted boiling water for just a minute to loosen the skins, then immerse them in ice water until cool. Using a small knife, pierce the skin of each bean opposite where it was attached to the pod and squeeze lightly. If fava beans are not available, try English peas or other shelling beans in this dish.

7–8 cups (56–64 fl oz/ 1.75–2 l) chicken stock (page 110)

¼ cup (2 fl oz/60 ml) extra-virgin olive oil

1 yellow onion, finely chopped

1 small carrot, peeled and finely chopped

1 celery stalk, finely chopped

3 cups (21 oz/655 g) Arborio or Carnaroli rice

1 cup (8 fl oz/250 ml) dry white wine, at room temperature

2 lb (1 kg) fava (broad) beans, shelled and skinned (far left)

1 tablespoon unsalted butter

¼ cup (1 oz/30 g) freshly grated Parmesan cheese

Salt and freshly ground pepper

RISOTTO WITH ARTICHOKES

6 baby artichokes, about 18 oz (560 g) total weight

1 lemon, cut in half

7–8 cups (56–64 fl oz/ 1.75–2 l) vegetable stock (page 111)

¼ cup (2 fl oz/60 ml) extra-virgin olive oil

½ cup (2½ oz/75 g) finely chopped yellow onion

2 carrots, peeled and diced

2 cloves garlic, thinly sliced

3 cups (21 oz/655 g) Arborio or Carnaroli rice

1 cup (8 fl oz/250 ml) dry white wine, at room temperature

2 tablespoons unsalted butter

1 cup (4 oz/125 g) freshly grated Parmesan cheese

Salt and freshly ground pepper

Trim the tops of the baby artichokes and remove any coarse outer leaves. Cut the artichokes in half lengthwise. Remove the fine center leaves and cut each half in half again lengthwise to create quarters. Rub all cut surfaces with the lemon halves. Set aside.

In a saucepan over medium heat, bring the stock to a gentle simmer and maintain over low heat.

In a large, heavy saucepan, heat the oil over medium heat. Add the onion, carrots, and garlic and cook until the onion is softened but not browned, about 4 minutes. Add the rice and stir until each grain is well coated with oil and translucent with a white dot in the center, about 3 minutes. Add the wine and stir until it is completely absorbed.

Add the artichokes, and then add the simmering stock a ladleful at a time, stirring frequently after each addition. Wait until the stock is almost completely absorbed (but the rice is never dry on top) before adding the next ladleful. Reserve ¼ cup (2 fl oz/60 ml) stock to add at the end.

When the rice is tender to the bite but slightly firm in the center and looks creamy and the artichokes are tender when pierced, after about 20 minutes, remove from the heat and stir in the butter, cheese, and reserved ¼ cup stock. Season to taste with salt and pepper and serve at once.

MAKES 6 SERVINGS

ARTICHOKE VARIATION

Baby artichokes, which are artichokes that grow lower on the stalk and do not reach full size or develop chokes, are tender and delicious, but the hearts of three or four full-size artichokes will also work nicely in this recipe. Trim off the stem and all the leaves, scraping away the fuzzy choke with a small knife. Cut the hearts into slices ½ inch (12 mm) thick and continue with the recipe.

RISOTTO WITH SPINACH

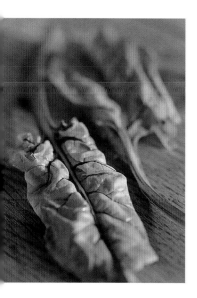

RISOTTO VERDE

Shredded spinach gives this risotto a lovely green hue. Other greens can make a delicious substitute; try Swiss chard, mustard greens, or turnip greens. To give a more even green color to the risotto, after sautéing the spinach or other greens, purée them with ¼ cup (2 fl oz/60 ml) vegetable stock in a food processor or blender.

In a saucepan over medium heat, bring the stock to a gentle simmer and maintain over low heat.

In a large, heavy saucepan, heat the oil over medium heat. Add the onion and sauté until softened, about 4 minutes. Add the spinach, reduce the heat to low, cover, and cook until tender, about 5 minutes. Using a slotted spoon, transfer the spinach mixture to a bowl and set aside.

Add the rice to the same pan and stir until each grain is well coated with oil and translucent with a white dot in the center, about 3 minutes. Add the wine and stir until it is completely absorbed.

Add the simmering stock a ladleful at a time, stirring frequently after each addition. Wait until the stock is almost completely absorbed (but the rice is never dry on top) before adding the next ladleful. Reserve ¼ cup (2 fl oz/60 ml) stock to add at the end.

When the rice is almost tender to the bite but slightly firm in the center and looks creamy, after about 18 minutes, return the spinach mixture to the pan and add a ladleful of stock. Cook, stirring occasionally, until the spinach mixture is heated through and the rice is al dente, 2–3 minutes longer. Remove from the heat and stir in the butter, cheese, and reserved ¼ cup stock. Season to taste with nutmeg, salt, and pepper and serve at once.

MAKES 6 SERVINGS

7–8 cups (56–64 fl oz/ 1.75–2 l) vegetable stock (page 111)

¼ cup (2 fl oz/60 ml) extra-virgin olive oil

½ cup (2½ oz/75 g) finely chopped yellow onion

1 lb (500 g) spinach, stemmed and thinly sliced crosswise

3 cups (21 oz/655 g) Arborio or Carnaroli rice

1 cup (8 fl oz/250 ml) dry white wine, at room temperature

2 tablespoons unsalted butter

3 tablespoons freshly grated Parmesan cheese

Freshly grated nutmeg

Salt and freshly ground pepper

RISOTTO CAPRESE

7–8 cups (56–64 fl oz/
1.75–2 l) chicken stock
(page 110)

¼ cup (2 fl oz/60 ml)
extra-virgin olive oil

½ cup (2½ oz/75 g) finely
chopped yellow onion

3 cups (21 oz/655 g)
Arborio or Carnaroli rice

1 cup (8 fl oz/250 ml)
dry white wine, at room
temperature

¾ lb (375 g) fresh
mozzarella cheese

2 cups (12 oz/375 g) cherry
tomatoes, stemmed and
halved

¼ cup (⅓ oz/10 g)
julienned fresh basil
leaves

Salt and freshly ground
pepper

In a saucepan over medium heat, bring the stock to a gentle simmer and maintain over low heat.

In a large, heavy saucepan, heat the oil over medium heat. Add the onion and sauté until softened, about 4 minutes. Add the rice and stir until each grain is well coated with oil and translucent with a white dot in the center, about 3 minutes. Add the wine and stir until it is completely absorbed.

Add the simmering stock a ladleful at a time, stirring frequently after each addition. Wait until the stock is almost completely absorbed (but the rice is never dry on top) before adding the next ladleful. Reserve ¼ cup (2 fl oz/60 ml) stock to add at the end.

If using 2-inch (5-cm) balls of mozzarella, cut them into slices ½ inch (12 mm) thick. Smaller balls may be left whole.

When the rice is tender to the bite but slightly firm in the center and looks creamy, after about 20 minutes, remove from the heat and stir in the reserved ¼ cup stock, the mozzarella, tomatoes, and basil. Season to taste with salt and pepper and serve at once.

MAKES 6 SERVINGS

FRESH MOZZARELLA
In southern Italy, the word *mozzarella* always means fresh mozzarella made from the milk of the water buffalo. When the same cheese is made with cow's milk, it is called *fior di latte*. Either is delicious in this supremely summery dish, inspired by the famous salad from the island of Capri that layers sliced sweet tomatoes with cool fresh mozzarella and fragrant basil leaves. When buying fresh mozzarella, look for 1-inch (2.5-cm) balls called *bocconcini* or larger 2-inch (5-cm) balls.

RISOTTO WITH RADICCHIO

In a saucepan over medium heat, bring the stock to a gentle simmer and maintain over low heat.

In a large, heavy saucepan, heat the oil over medium heat. Add the pancetta and sauté until golden brown, 4–5 minutes. Add the onion and sauté until just softened, 2–3 minutes. Add the thinly sliced radicchio and sauté until tender, about 2 minutes. Using a slotted spoon, transfer the radicchio mixture to a bowl. Set aside and keep warm.

Add the rice to the same pan and stir until each grain is well coated with oil and translucent with a white dot in the center, about 3 minutes. Add the wine and stir until it is completely absorbed.

Add the simmering stock a ladleful at a time, stirring frequently after each addition. Wait until the stock is almost completely absorbed (but the rice is never dry on top) before adding the next ladleful. Reserve ¼ cup (2 fl oz/60 ml) stock to add at the end.

When the rice is tender to the bite but slightly firm in the center and looks creamy, after about 20 minutes, remove from the heat and stir in the butter and reserved ¼ cup stock. Season to taste with salt and pepper. Place 2 Verona radicchio leaves on each plate. Spoon the risotto into the leaves. Make a well in the center and spoon in the radicchio mixture. Serve at once.

MAKES 6 SERVINGS

7–8 cups (56–64 fl oz/ 1.75–2 l) chicken stock (page 110)

¼ cup (2 fl oz/60 ml) extra-virgin olive oil

3 oz (90 g) pancetta, finely chopped

½ cup (2½ oz/75 g) finely chopped yellow onion

2 heads Treviso or Verona radicchio, thinly sliced crosswise, plus 12 small whole Verona radicchio leaves for serving

3 cups (21 oz/655 g) Arborio or Carnaroli rice

1 cup (8 fl oz/250 ml) dry white wine, at room temperature

2 tablespoons unsalted butter

Salt and freshly ground pepper

RISOTTO WITH ROASTED BUTTERNUT SQUASH

1 butternut squash, about 1½ lb (750 g)

7–8 cups (56–64 fl oz/ 1.75–2 l) chicken stock (page 110)

¼ cup (2 fl oz/60 ml) extra-virgin olive oil

½ cup (2½ oz/75 g) finely chopped yellow onion

3 cups (21 oz/655 g) Arborio or Carnaroli rice

1 cup (8 fl oz/250 ml) dry white wine, at room temperature

2 tablespoons unsalted butter

Salt and freshly ground pepper

Preheat the oven to 400°F (200°C). Lightly oil a shallow baking dish. Cut the butternut squash in half lengthwise. Scoop out the seeds and discard. Place cut side down on a baking sheet and bake until very soft, 35–45 minutes. Remove from the oven and let cool to the touch. Scoop out the flesh and purée in a blender or food processor. Set aside.

In a saucepan over medium heat, bring the stock to a gentle simmer and maintain over low heat.

In a large, heavy saucepan, heat the oil over medium heat. Add the onion and sauté until softened, about 4 minutes. Add the rice and stir until each grain is well coated with oil and translucent with a white dot in the center, about 3 minutes. Add the wine and stir until it is completely absorbed.

Add the simmering stock a ladleful at a time, stirring frequently after each addition. Wait until the stock is almost completely absorbed (but the rice is never dry on top) before adding the next ladleful. Reserve ¼ cup (2 fl oz/60 ml) stock to add at the end.

When the rice is tender to the bite but slightly firm in the center and looks creamy, after about 20 minutes, stir in the squash purée. Cook to heat through, about 30 seconds. Remove from the heat and stir in the butter and reserved ¼ cup stock. Season to taste with salt and pepper and serve at once.

MAKES 6 SERVINGS

ROASTING VEGETABLES

Roasting sweetens squash by caramelizing its naturally occurring sugars and softens the flesh so that it can be puréed and stirred into this risotto. Other vegetables that would work well in this recipe are zucchini (courgettes), eggplant (aubergine), and beets. Use a hot oven and roast the vegetables until very tender, adjusting the cooking time according to the density of the vegetable; coarse winter squash will take longer than zucchini, for example.

RISOTTO WITH LEEKS AND SUN-DRIED TOMATOES

In a saucepan over medium heat, bring the stock to a gentle simmer and maintain over low heat.

In a large, heavy saucepan, heat the oil over medium heat. Add the leeks and bell pepper and sauté until softened, about 4 minutes. Using a slotted spoon, transfer the leek mixture to a bowl and set aside.

Add the rice to the same pan and stir until each grain is well coated with oil and translucent with a white dot in the center, about 3 minutes. Add the wine and stir until it is completely absorbed.

Add the simmering stock a ladleful at a time, stirring frequently after each addition. Wait until the stock is almost completely absorbed (but the rice is never dry on top) before adding the next ladleful. Reserve ¼ cup (2 fl oz/60 ml) stock to add at the end.

When the rice is tender to the bite but slightly firm in the center and looks creamy, after about 20 minutes, stir in the leek mixture and sun-dried tomatoes. Cook to heat through, about 30 seconds. Remove from the heat and stir in the butter and reserved ¼ cup stock. Season to taste with salt and pepper and serve at once.

MAKES 6 SERVINGS

LEEKS

Sweet and mild, leeks give this risotto a base of rich flavor that differs slightly from that of onions, which are more typically used. To clean a leek, trim off the root and tough green top and cut the stalk in half lengthwise. Rinse under cold running water, spreading the layers apart to wash away any grit. For this recipe, thinly slice the leeks crosswise.

7–8 cups (56–64 fl oz/ 1.75–2 l) chicken stock (page 110)

¼ cup (2 fl oz/60 ml) extra-virgin olive oil

3 leeks, white part only, carefully rinsed and thinly sliced crosswise *(far left)*

1 yellow bell pepper (capsicum), seeded and cut into ½-inch (12-mm) chunks

3 cups (21 oz/655 g) Arborio or Carnaroli rice

1 cup (8 fl oz/250 ml) dry white wine, at room temperature

½ cup (3 oz/90 g) drained oil-packed sun-dried tomatoes, julienned

2 tablespoons unsalted butter

Salt and freshly ground pepper

RISOTTO WITH BEETS

8 small or 3 large beets
with greens

3 cups (24 fl oz/750 ml)
water

Salt and freshly ground
pepper

6 tablespoons (3 fl oz/
90 ml) extra-virgin
olive oil

4–5 cups (32–40 fl oz/
1–1.25 l) chicken stock
(page 110)

½ cup (2½ oz/75 g) finely
chopped yellow onion

3 cups (21 oz/655 g)
Arborio or Carnaroli rice

1 cup (8 fl oz/250 ml)
dry white wine, at room
temperature

2 tablespoons unsalted
butter

Preheat the oven to 400°F (200°C). Lightly oil a baking dish. Remove the beet greens and discard the tough stems. Rinse the greens and spin dry, then thinly slice the leaves crosswise and set aside. Trim the root and stem from the beets and scrub well. Quarter small beets lengthwise, or cut large beets into chunks. In a saucepan, bring the water to a boil and add salt to taste. Add the beets and cook until fork tender, 8–12 minutes. Drain, reserving the water, and remove the skins. Put the beets in the prepared baking dish and drizzle with 2 tablespoons of the oil. Season to taste with salt and pepper. Roast until lightly browned, about 20 minutes. Set aside.

In a saucepan over medium heat, combine the stock and beet liquid. Bring to a gentle simmer and maintain over low heat.

In a large, heavy saucepan over medium heat, heat the remaining 4 tablespoons (2 fl oz/60 ml) oil. Add the onion and sauté until softened, about 4 minutes. Add the greens from the beets and sauté until softened, about 3 minutes. With a slotted spoon, transfer the greens mixture to a bowl and set aside. Add the rice to the pan and stir until each grain is well coated with oil and translucent with a white dot in the center, about 3 minutes. Add the wine and stir until it is completely absorbed.

Add the hot stock mixture a ladleful at a time, stirring frequently after each addition. Wait until the stock is almost completely absorbed (but the rice is never dry on top) before adding the next ladleful. Reserve ¼ cup (2 fl oz/60 ml) stock to add at the end.

When the rice is tender to the bite but slightly firm in the center and looks creamy, after about 20 minutes, stir in the beets and greens. Cook to heat through, about 1 minute. Remove from the heat and stir in the butter and reserved ¼ cup stock. Season to taste with salt and pepper and serve at once.

MAKES 6 SERVINGS

ADDING COLOR

In some recipes, keeping bright red beets from "bleeding" and staining other ingredients is a concern. In this recipe, the beets' brilliant magenta color is as desirable as their earthy, sweet flavor. If you like the effect, try using other puréed brightly colored vegetables, such as carrots or roasted red or yellow bell peppers (capsicums), to give your risottos a dramatic flair.

SEAFOOD RISOTTOS

Seafood risottos can be surprisingly delicate and refined. The rice provides a perfect backdrop for both shellfish and fish. Many of these recipes come from the Veneto, where the markets teem with seafood from the Adriatic Sea. But other regional specialties are also included, such as a sautéed shrimp risotto flavored with Ligurian pesto.

RISOTTO WITH PESTO AND SHRIMP
46

RISOTTO WITH SALMON AND DILL
49

RISOTTO WITH SQUID INK
50

RISOTTO WITH SEA BASS AND FENNEL
53

RISOTTO WITH SAUTÉED SCALLOPS
54

RISOTTO WITH LOBSTER
57

RISOTTO WITH PESTO AND SHRIMP

To make the pesto, purée the garlic in a mini food processor or blender. Add the basil and pine nuts and process to a grainy texture. With the machine running, gradually add the oil. The pesto will be quite thick. Pour into a bowl and stir in the cheese. Set aside.

In a saucepan over medium heat, bring the stock to a gentle simmer and maintain over low heat.

In a large, heavy saucepan, heat the oil over medium heat. Add the onion and sauté until softened, about 4 minutes. Add the shrimp and sauté until firm and pink, 4–5 minutes. Using a slotted spoon, transfer the shrimp mixture to a bowl and set aside.

Add the rice to the same pan and stir until each grain is well coated with oil and translucent with a white dot in the center, about 3 minutes. Add the wine and stir until it is completely absorbed.

Add the simmering stock a ladleful at a time, stirring frequently after each addition. Wait until the stock is almost completely absorbed (but the rice is never dry on top) before adding the next ladleful. Reserve ¼ cup (2 fl oz/60 ml) stock to add at the end.

When the rice is tender to the bite but slightly firm in the center and looks creamy, after about 20 minutes, stir in the shrimp. Cook to heat through, about 1 minute. Remove from the heat and stir in 2–4 tablespoons pesto, or to taste, and the reserved ¼ cup stock. Season to taste with salt and pepper and serve at once.

MAKES 6 SERVINGS

USES FOR PESTO

This basic pesto recipe can be used in a variety of ways in addition to stirring it into risotto. Add a couple more tablespoons of olive oil to thin it enough to use for saucing pasta. To use as a marinade for poultry or seafood, decrease the oil to 3 tablespoons. Or mix in ¼ lb (125 g) cream cheese, at room temperature, for a delicious dip for raw vegetables. You can also swirl a dollop of pesto into a bowl of hot minestrone for added flavor.

FOR THE PESTO:

3 cloves garlic

Leaves from 1 bunch fresh basil

¼ cup (1 oz/30 g) pine nuts, toasted (page 72)

¼ cup (2 fl oz/60 ml) extra-virgin olive oil

¼ cup (1 oz/30 g) freshly grated Parmesan cheese

7–8 cups (56–64 fl oz/ 1.75–2 l) shellfish stock (page 111)

¼ cup (2 fl oz/60 ml) extra-virgin olive oil

½ cup (2½ oz/75 g) finely chopped yellow onion

½ lb (250 g) shrimp (prawns), peeled and deveined (page 115)

3 cups (21 oz/655 g) Arborio or Carnaroli rice

1 cup (8 fl oz/250 ml) dry white wine, at room temperature

Salt and freshly ground pepper

RISOTTO WITH SALMON AND DILL

1 lb (500 g) salmon fillet, cut into 6 equal pieces

Salt and freshly ground pepper

7–8 cups (56–64 fl oz/ 1.75–2 l) fish stock (page 111)

¼ cup (2 fl oz/60 ml) extra-virgin olive oil

¼ cup (1 oz/30 g) finely chopped green (spring) onion, including tender green tops

3 cups (21 oz/655 g) Arborio or Carnaroli rice

1 cup (8 fl oz/250 ml) Prosecco, other sparkling wine, or dry white wine, at room temperature

2 tablespoons unsalted butter

Dill sprigs for garnish

Preheat the oven to 375°F (190°C). Lightly oil a baking dish. Check the salmon for any stray pin bones and remove them with tweezers or needle-nosed pliers. Place the salmon in the prepared dish and season to taste with salt and pepper. Bake the salmon, turning once, until opaque and firm to the touch, 3–5 minutes on each side depending on the thickness of the fillet. Remove from the oven. Set aside and keep warm.

Meanwhile, start the risotto. In a saucepan over medium heat, bring the stock to a gentle simmer and maintain over low heat.

In a large, heavy saucepan, heat the oil over medium heat. Add the green onion and sauté until softened, 2–3 minutes. Add the rice and stir until each grain is well coated with oil and translucent with a white dot in the center, about 3 minutes. Add the wine and stir until it is completely absorbed.

Add the simmering stock a ladleful at a time, stirring frequently after each addition. Wait until the stock is almost completely absorbed (but the rice is never dry on top) before adding the next ladleful. Reserve ¼ cup (2 fl oz/60 ml) stock to add at the end.

When the rice is tender to the bite but slightly firm in the center and looks creamy, after about 20 minutes, remove from the heat and stir in the butter and reserved ¼ cup stock. Season to taste with salt and pepper. Divide the risotto evenly among warmed shallow bowls and place a piece of salmon on top of each serving. Sprinkle with the dill sprigs and serve at once.

MAKES 6 SERVINGS

PROSECCO

This type of sparkling wine is traditionally made from the Prosecco grape, which grows in the Veneto, in northeastern Italy, although up to 15 percent of the juice can be from Pinot Bianco grapes or a mixture of Pinot Grigio and Chardonnay. The most famous Prosecco wines are produced in the towns of Conegliano and Valdobbiadene. While the wine is most often thought of as an element in a cocktail—combined with peach purée to create the Bellini—its delicate flavor is also used in the cooking of the area. Any sparkling white wine, including Champagne, can be used in its place.

RISOTTO WITH SQUID INK

In a saucepan over medium heat, bring the stock to a gentle simmer and maintain over low heat.

In a large, heavy saucepan, heat the oil over medium heat. Add the onion and sauté until softened, about 4 minutes. Add the rice and stir until each grain is well coated with oil and translucent with a white dot in the center, about 3 minutes. Add the wine and stir until it is completely absorbed.

Add the simmering stock a ladleful at a time, stirring frequently after each addition. Wait until the stock is almost completely absorbed (but the rice is never dry on top) before adding the next ladleful. Reserve ¼ cup (2 fl oz/60 ml) stock to add at the end.

When the rice is tender to the bite but slightly firm in the center and looks creamy, after about 20 minutes, remove from the heat and stir in the butter, squid ink, and reserved ¼ cup stock. Season to taste with salt and pepper and serve at once.

MAKES 6 SERVINGS

7–8 cups (56–64 fl oz/ 1.75–2 l) fish stock (page 111)

¼ cup (2 fl oz/60 ml) extra-virgin olive oil

½ cup (2½ oz/75 g) finely chopped yellow onion

3 cups (21 oz/655 g) Arborio or Carnaroli rice

1 cup (8 fl oz/250 ml) dry white wine, at room temperature

2 tablespoons unsalted butter

2 teaspoons squid ink

Salt and freshly ground pepper

SQUID AND ITS INK

In Italy, this dish would be made with the ink of the cuttlefish, a relative of squid. When you buy cuttlefish or squid in Italy, they come with their sacs of black ink intact. Elsewhere, look for squid ink in little packets at fishmongers and Italian food stores. Whether or not you are able to find the ink, you can add squid to this recipe. Sauté 1 lb (500 g) cleaned fresh squid, cut into ½-inch (12-mm) pieces, in 3 tablespoons olive oil with ½ yellow onion, chopped, and 1 clove garlic, minced. Add dry white wine to cover and simmer until tender, about 30 minutes. Stir into the risotto just before serving.

RISOTTO WITH SEA BASS AND FENNEL

7–8 cups (56–64 fl oz/
1.75–2 l) fish stock
(page 111)

3 tablespoons unsalted
butter

2 tablespoons extra-virgin
olive oil

⅓ cup (1½ oz/45 g) finely
chopped yellow onion

1 celery stalk, finely
chopped

1 clove garlic, minced

¾ lb (375 g) sea bass fillet,
cut into 2-inch (5-cm)
chunks

3 cups (21 oz/655 g)
Arborio or Carnaroli rice

1 cup (8 fl oz/250 ml)
dry white wine, at room
temperature

1 small fennel bulb,
trimmed and thinly sliced,
fronds reserved for garnish

Salt and freshly ground
pepper

In a saucepan over medium heat, bring the stock to a gentle simmer and maintain over low heat.

In a large, heavy saucepan over medium heat, melt 2 tablespoons of the butter with the oil. Add the onion, celery, and garlic and sauté until softened, about 4 minutes. Add the sea bass and sauté until firm and opaque, 4–5 minutes. Using a slotted spoon, transfer the sea bass mixture to a bowl and set aside.

Add the rice to the same pan and stir until each grain is well coated with oil and translucent with a white dot in the center, about 3 minutes. Add the wine and stir until it is completely absorbed.

Stir in the fennel slices. Add the simmering stock a ladleful at a time, stirring frequently after each addition. Wait until the stock is almost completely absorbed (but the rice is never dry on top) before adding the next ladleful. Reserve ¼ cup (2 fl oz/60 ml) stock to add at the end.

When the rice is tender to the bite but slightly firm in the center and looks creamy, after about 20 minutes, gently stir in the sea bass, the reserved ¼ cup stock, and the remaining 1 tablespoon butter. Cook to heat through, about 1 minute. Season to taste with salt and pepper and spoon into warmed shallow bowls. Garnish with fennel fronds and serve at once.

MAKES 6 SERVINGS

FENNEL

Fennel, known as *finocchio* in Italian, is a versatile bulb available from late autumn until early spring. Its flavor is sweet and faintly reminiscent of anise or licorice. Fennel is excellent sliced thin and served raw in salads, roasted alongside meats, or slowly braised in liquid, as in this recipe. Trim off the stalks and reserve the feathery fronds to use as a garnish.

RISOTTO WITH SAUTÉED SCALLOPS

In a saucepan over medium heat, bring the stock to a gentle simmer and maintain over low heat.

In a large, heavy saucepan, heat the oil over medium heat. Add the onion and sauté until softened, about 4 minutes. Add the lemon zest and cook until fragrant, about 1 minute. Add the scallops and cook until firm and opaque, 1–2 minutes. Using a slotted spoon, transfer the scallop mixture to a bowl and set aside.

Add the rice to the same pan and stir until each grain is well coated with oil and translucent with a white dot in the center, about 3 minutes. Add the wine and stir until it is completely absorbed.

Add the minced tarragon to the simmering stock. Add the stock to the rice a ladleful at a time, stirring frequently after each addition. Wait until the stock is almost completely absorbed (but the rice is never dry on top) before adding the next ladleful. Reserve ¼ cup (2 fl oz/60 ml) stock to add at the end.

When the rice is tender to the bite but slightly firm in the center and looks creamy, after about 20 minutes, gently stir in the scallops, butter, and reserved ¼ cup stock. Cook to heat through, about 1 minute. Season to taste with salt and pepper and spoon into warmed shallow bowls. Garnish with tarragon sprigs and serve immediately.

MAKES 6 SERVINGS

ZESTING CITRUS

The brightly colored outer peel of citrus contains essential oils that enhance many dishes, both savory and sweet. Use a fine grater or zester to remove only the brightly colored zest, leaving behind the bitter white pith. A swivel-bladed vegetable peeler can also be used to remove wider strips, which can then be minced with a sharp knife.

7–8 cups (56–64 fl oz/1.75–2 l) shellfish stock (page 111)

¼ cup (2 fl oz/60 ml) extra-virgin olive oil

½ cup (2½ oz/75 g) finely chopped yellow onion

Grated zest of 1 lemon *(far left)*

¾ lb (375 g) sea scallops

3 cups (21 oz/655 g) Arborio or Carnaroli rice

1 cup (8 fl oz/250 ml) dry white wine, at room temperature

1 teaspoon minced fresh tarragon, plus sprigs for garnish

2 tablespoons unsalted butter

Salt and freshly ground pepper

RISOTTO WITH LOBSTER

7–8 cups (56–64 fl oz/
1.75–2 l) shellfish stock
(page 111)

4 fresh tarragon sprigs

3 lobster tails, about 2½ lb
(1.25 kg) total weight

¼ cup (2 fl oz/60 ml)
extra-virgin olive oil

½ cup (2½ oz/75 g) finely
chopped yellow onion

3 cups (21 oz/655 g)
Arborio or Carnaroli rice

1 cup (8 fl oz/250 ml)
Prosecco, other sparkling
wine, or dry white wine,
at room temperature

3 tablespoons unsalted
butter

Salt and freshly ground
pepper

2 tablespoons Sevruga
caviar (optional)

In a large soup pot, bring the stock to a boil. Add the tarragon and lobster tails and cook until the lobster shells are bright red, 4–5 minutes. Using a skimmer, transfer the tarragon and lobster to a plate, maintaining the stock at a gentle simmer over low heat. When the lobster has cooled to the touch, remove the shells and cut the lobster meat into 1-inch (2.5-cm) pieces. Set aside.

In a large, heavy saucepan, heat the oil over medium heat. Add the onion and sauté until softened, about 4 minutes. Add the rice and stir until each grain is well coated with oil and translucent with a white dot at the center, about 3 minutes. Add the wine and stir until it is completely absorbed.

Add the simmering stock a ladleful at a time, stirring frequently after each addition. Wait until the stock is almost completely absorbed (but the rice is never dry on top) before adding the next ladleful. Reserve ¼ cup (2 fl oz/60 ml) stock to add at the end.

When the rice is tender to the bite but slightly firm in the center and looks creamy, after about 20 minutes, gently stir in the lobster pieces. Cook to heat through, about 30 seconds. Remove from the heat and stir in the butter and reserved ¼ cup stock. Season to taste with salt and pepper and spoon into warmed shallow bowls. Garnish with caviar, if desired, and serve at once.

Serving Tip: Prepare this recipe as a stunning first course for a dinner party, or for a more impressive main course, serve the risotto with whole lobster tails (right).

MAKES 6 SERVINGS

LOBSTER TAILS

Lobster tails are an easy route to an elegant meal. The tails, which are sold frozen, are typically those of spiny, or rock, lobsters, which have only small legs and lack the large claws of the meat-rich Maine lobster. They do, however, carry plump, firm, tasty meat that complements risottos and other dishes. Buy lobster tails at a good-quality fishmonger where you are assured of a high-end product. For a more dramatic presentation for this dish, buy 6 tails, cook as directed, and then remove the shells, leaving the tail meat intact. Place a whole tail atop each serving of risotto.

POULTRY AND MEAT RISOTTOS

From risottos made with roasted chicken or sautéed duck to ones enriched with prosciutto, sausage, lamb, or beef, the offerings in this chapter make for hearty main dishes. Try a few, then keep risotto in mind as an excellent way to use roasted poultry or grilled meat, inventing your own dish next time.

RISOTTO WITH CHICKEN
AND CARAMELIZED ONIONS

In a large, heavy saucepan, heat ¼ cup (2 fl oz/60 ml) of the oil over medium-high heat. Add the onions and leek and sauté until the onions turn golden brown, about 15 minutes. Add the Madeira and deglaze the pan, stirring to scrape up the browned bits from the bottom. Cook over medium-high heat to reduce the liquid by half. Meanwhile, in a saucepan over medium heat, bring the stock to a gentle simmer and maintain over low heat. Add 1 cup (8 fl oz/250 ml) of the simmering stock to the onion mixture and continue to cook over medium-high heat until the liquid has reduced and the mixture is quite thick, about 15 minutes longer. Set aside.

While the onions simmer, in another large, heavy saucepan, heat the remaining ¼ cup olive oil over medium heat. Add the rice and stir until each grain is well coated with oil and translucent with a white dot in the center, about 3 minutes.

Add the simmering stock a ladleful at a time, stirring frequently after each addition. Wait until the stock is almost completely absorbed (but the rice is never dry on top) before adding the next ladleful. Reserve ¼ cup (2 fl oz/60 ml) stock to add at the end.

When the rice is tender to the bite but slightly firm in the center and looks creamy, after about 20 minutes, stir in the chicken. Cook to heat through, about 1 minute. Remove from the heat and stir in the butter, caramelized onion mixture, and reserved ¼ cup stock. Season to taste with salt and pepper and serve at once.

Note: Use leftover roasted chicken or poached chicken breasts. To poach chicken breasts, put 2–3 bone-in breast halves in a large saucepan and add lightly salted water to cover. Bring to a boil over high heat. Reduce the heat to low and simmer for 30 minutes.

MAKES 6 SERVINGS

CARAMELIZED ONIONS
Onions are naturally high in sugar. Some varieties, such as California Red, Maui, Vidalia, and Walla Walla, taste especially sweet even when raw. When these or other onions are cooked to a golden brown, their natural sugars melt and start to caramelize, giving them a delicious flavor with no trace of acidity.

½ cup (4 fl oz/125 ml) extra-virgin olive oil

2 sweet white onions, cut into 1-inch (2.5-cm) pieces

1 leek, white part only, cut into 1-inch (2.5-cm) pieces

1 cup (8 fl oz/250 ml) Madeira wine, at room temperature

9–10 cups (72–80 fl oz/ 2.25–2.5 l) chicken stock (page 110)

3 cups (21 oz/655 g) Arborio or Carnaroli rice

2 cups (12 oz/375 g) chopped cooked chicken meat (see Note)

2 tablespoons unsalted butter

Salt and freshly ground pepper

BALSAMIC RISOTTO WITH ROASTED CHICKEN

FOR THE CHICKEN:

4 tablespoons (2 fl oz/ 60 ml) extra-virgin olive oil, plus extra for coating

8 cloves garlic

1 tablespoon good-quality balsamic vinegar of Modena *(far right)*

3 tablespoons minced fresh flat-leaf (Italian) parsley

1 chicken, about 2½ lb (1.25 kg)

Salt and freshly ground pepper

FOR THE RISOTTO:

7–8 cups (56–64 fl oz/ 1.75–2 l) chicken stock (page 110)

¼ cup (2 fl oz/60 ml) extra-virgin olive oil

½ cup (2½ oz/75 g) finely chopped yellow onion

3 cups (21 oz/655 g) Arborio or Carnaroli rice

½ cup (4 fl oz/125 ml) good-quality balsamic vinegar of Modena

2 tablespoons unsalted butter

Salt and freshly ground pepper

To prepare the chicken, preheat the oven to 400°F (200°C). Pour 3 tablespoons of the oil into a roasting pan. Mince 4 cloves of the garlic. In a small bowl, combine the minced garlic, balsamic vinegar, the remaining 1 tablespoon oil, and the parsley.

Beginning at the neck, loosen the skin from the chicken breast with your fingers. Spread the garlic mixture over the breast under the skin. Place the whole garlic cloves in the cavity. Rub the skin with oil, season with salt and pepper, and place the bird on its side in the pan. Roast, turning from side to side every 15 minutes and occasionally basting with the pan juices, until the juices run clear when a thigh is pierced, 45–60 minutes. Turn breast side up for the last 15 minutes to brown. Transfer to a plate, reserving the pan juices, and let cool to the touch. Remove the meat from the bones and cut into bite-sized pieces.

Meanwhile, start the risotto. In a saucepan over medium heat, bring the stock to a gentle simmer and maintain over low heat. In a large, heavy saucepan, heat the oil over medium heat. Add the onion and sauté until softened, about 4 minutes. Add the rice and stir until each grain is well coated with oil and translucent with a white dot in the center, about 3 minutes. Add the balsamic vinegar and stir until it is completely absorbed. Add the simmering stock a ladleful at a time, stirring frequently after each addition. Wait until the stock is almost completely absorbed (but the rice is never dry on top) before adding the next ladleful. Reserve ¼ cup (2 fl oz/60 ml) stock to add at the end.

When the rice is tender to the bite but slightly firm in the center and looks creamy, after about 20 minutes, stir in the roasted chicken. Cook to heat through, about 1 minute. Remove from the heat and stir in the butter and reserved ¼ cup stock. Season to taste with salt and pepper and serve at once.

MAKES 6 SERVINGS

BALSAMIC STYLES

Aceto balsamico tradizionale, or traditional balsamic vinegar, comes from the Italian region of Emilia-Romagna. Traditional balsamic is made from cooked grapes that are aged in barrels of a variety of woods for a minimum of twelve years. The final product is slightly thick and should never be cooked. Balsamic vinegar of Modena, used in this recipe, is made by the same process but aged for a shorter time and is delicious in its own way. Use it to dress salads and to add a caramelized, savory flavor to cooked foods.

RISOTTO WITH DUCK AND BLOOD ORANGES

SEGMENTING ORANGES

Blood oranges are popular for their intense flavor and amazing color, which can range from ruby red to almost black. Their short season is in winter; when they are not available, substitute navel or Valencia oranges. To peel and segment an orange or other citrus fruit neatly, cut a slice off the top and bottom of the fruit down to the flesh, then stand it upright. Following the contour of the fruit, slice off the peel and white pith in thick strips down to the flesh. Holding the fruit over a bowl, slice on either side of each membrane to release the segments into the bowl.

Preheat the oven to 400°F (200°C). Using a sharp knife, score the duck skin in a crosshatch pattern, taking care not to cut into the meat. Season the duck breast halves with salt and pepper.

Place the duck breasts, skin side down, in an unheated, large non-stick frying pan with an ovenproof handle. Place over medium heat and cook until the skin is golden brown, about 10 minutes. (Don't preheat the pan; gradual heating will render the most fat.) Pour off the accumulated fat from the pan. Turn the breasts over and immediately transfer the pan to the oven. Roast until medium-rare (somewhat soft with a bit of resilience when pressed in the center), about 10 minutes. Set aside and keep warm.

Meanwhile, in a saucepan over medium heat, bring the stock to a gentle simmer and maintain over low heat. In a large, heavy saucepan, heat the oil over medium heat. Add the shallots and sauté until softened, 3–4 minutes. Add the rice and stir until each grain is well coated with oil and translucent with a white dot in the center, about 3 minutes. Add the wine and orange zest and stir until the wine is completely absorbed.

Add the simmering stock a ladleful at a time, stirring frequently after each addition. Wait until the stock is almost completely absorbed (but the rice is never dry on top) before adding the next ladleful. Reserve ¼ cup (2 fl oz/60 ml) stock to add at the end.

When the rice is tender to the bite but slightly firm in the center and looks creamy, after about 20 minutes, remove from the heat and stir in the butter and the reserved ¼ cup stock. Season to taste with salt and pepper. Spoon the risotto into warmed shallow bowls. Thickly slice each duck breast half crosswise and arrange on top of a serving of risotto. Garnish with the orange sections and serve at once.

MAKES 6 SERVINGS

6 boneless duck breast halves, about 2 lb (1 kg), trimmed

Salt and freshly ground pepper

7–8 cups (56–64 fl oz/ 1.75–2 l) chicken stock (page 110)

3 tablespoons extra-virgin olive oil

2 shallots, minced

3 cups (21 oz/655 g) Arborio or Carnaroli rice

1 cup (8 fl oz/250 ml) dry white wine, at room temperature

Grated zest of 1 blood orange, plus 3 blood oranges, peeled and sectioned (far left)

2 tablespoons unsalted butter

RISOTTO RUSTICA
WITH PROSCIUTTO AND ARUGULA

7–8 cups (56–64 fl oz/
1.75–2 l) chicken stock
(page 110)

¼ cup (2 fl oz/60 ml)
extra-virgin olive oil

½ cup (2½ oz/75 g) finely
chopped yellow onion

3 cups (21 oz/655 g)
Arborio or Carnaroli rice

1 cup (8 fl oz/250 ml)
dry white wine, at room
temperature

2 tablespoons unsalted
butter

Salt and freshly ground
pepper

6 large, thin slices
prosciutto

1 bunch arugula, stemmed

Parmesan cheese for
serving

In a saucepan over medium heat, bring the stock to a gentle
simmer and maintain over low heat.

In a large, heavy saucepan, heat the oil over medium heat. Add
the onion and sauté until softened, about 4 minutes. Add the rice
and stir until each grain is well coated with oil and translucent
with a white dot in the center, about 3 minutes. Add the wine and
stir until it is completely absorbed.

Add the simmering stock a ladleful at a time, stirring frequently
after each addition. Wait until the stock is almost completely
absorbed (but the rice is never dry on top) before adding the next
ladleful. Reserve ¼ cup (2 fl oz/60 ml) stock to add at the end.

When the rice is tender to the bite but slightly firm in the center
and looks creamy, after about 20 minutes, remove from the heat
and stir in the butter and reserved ¼ cup stock. Season to taste
with salt and pepper. Line warmed shallow individual bowls with
prosciutto slices. Top with the risotto. Make a well in the risotto
and fill with the arugula, tearing large leaves into bite-sized
pieces. Using a vegetable peeler, shave paper-thin slices of cheese
over the top. Serve at once.

*Serving Tip: The elegant way in which this risotto is served—in bowls
lined with prosciutto and then topped with arugula and shaved
Parmesan cheese—makes it an excellent choice for a colorful and
delicious first course at a dinner party.*

MAKES 6 SERVINGS

PROSCIUTTO

Neither smoked nor cooked,
prosciutto is the rear leg of a
pig that has been seasoned,
salt-cured, and then air-dried
to make a prized Italian ham.
Every region makes its own
version, but the two most
famous are *prosciutto di
Parma* and *prosciutto di San
Daniele.* Here, thinly sliced
prosciutto provides a savory
contrast to the peppery
arugula and creamy risotto.
Any variety of prosciutto will
work well in this recipe.

RISOTTO WITH SAUSAGE AND FENNEL

Prepare a fire in a charcoal grill or preheat a broiler (grill). Lightly coat the sausages with oil and grill or broil them until nicely browned, about 5 minutes on each side. Transfer the sausages to a plate and let cool to the touch. Cut into 2 inch (5 cm) slices on the diagonal. Set aside.

In a saucepan over medium heat, bring the stock to a gentle simmer and maintain over low heat.

In a large, heavy saucepan, heat the ¼ cup oil over medium heat. Add the onion and fennel and sauté until softened, about 4 minutes. Add the rice and stir until each grain is well coated with oil and translucent with a white dot in the center, about 3 minutes. Add the wine and stir until it is completely absorbed.

Add the simmering stock a ladleful at a time, stirring frequently after each addition. Wait until the stock is almost completely absorbed (but the rice is never dry on top) before adding the next ladleful. Reserve ¼ cup (2 fl oz/60 ml) stock to add at the end.

When the rice is tender to the bite but slightly firm in the center and looks creamy, after about 20 minutes, add the bell peppers and sausages. Cook, stirring occasionally, to heat through, 1–2 minutes. Remove from the heat and stir in the butter and reserved ¼ cup stock. Season to taste with salt and pepper and serve at once.

MAKES 6 SERVINGS

ITALIAN SAUSAGES

Sausages, which in many cultures evolved from the need to salvage every shred of meat—often utilizing cuts less appealing in their whole form—have today become an art form. A wide range of herbs, spices, and other flavorings are used to give these old-fashioned supper staples a contemporary profile. In Italy, however, the simplest versions are still preferred, usually a choice of sweet or spicy. This recipe will work well with any variety of sausage.

4–6 sweet or hot Italian sausages, about 1 lb (500 g) total weight

7–8 cups (56–64 fl oz/ 1.75–2 l) chicken stock (page 110)

¼ cup (2 fl oz/60 ml) extra-virgin olive oil, plus extra for coating

½ cup (2½ oz/75 g) finely chopped yellow onion

1 medium fennel bulb, trimmed and coarsely chopped

3 cups (21 oz/655 g) Arborio or Carnaroli rice

1 cup (8 fl oz/250 ml) dry white wine, at room temperature

2 red bell peppers (capsicums), roasted and peeled (page 113), then seeded and julienned

2 yellow bell peppers (capsicums), roasted and peeled (page 113), then seeded and julienned

2 tablespoons unsalted butter

Salt and freshly ground pepper

RISOTTO WITH LAMB, ROSEMARY, AND OLIVES

1 lb (500 g) boneless lamb sirloin, cut into 1-inch (2.5-cm) cubes

Salt and freshly ground pepper

½ cup (4 fl oz/125 ml) extra-virgin olive oil

1 small yellow onion, thinly sliced, plus ½ cup (2½ oz/75 g) finely chopped

2 cups (16 fl oz/500 ml) dry red wine, at room temperature

9–10 cups (72–80 fl oz/ 2.25–2.5 l) meat stock (page 110)

1 can (14½ oz/455 g) whole tomatoes, with juice

1 tablespoon minced fresh flat-leaf (Italian) parsley

3 fresh rosemary sprigs

½ cup (2 oz/60 g) pitted Mediterranean black olives

3 cups (21 oz/655 g) Arborio or Carnaroli rice

2 tablespoons unsalted butter

Season the lamb cubes with salt and pepper. In a large frying pan, heat ¼ cup (2 fl oz/60 ml) of the oil over medium-high heat. Add the lamb cubes and sliced onion and cook until the lamb is browned on all sides, 8–10 minutes. With the meat and onion still in the pan, add 1 cup (8 fl oz/250 ml) of the wine and deglaze the pan, stirring to scrape up the browned bits from the bottom. Cook over high heat to reduce the liquid by half. Add 2 cups (16 fl oz/ 500 ml) of the stock and the tomatoes with their juices and return to a boil. Reduce the heat to medium and add the parsley and rosemary. Simmer, uncovered, until the lamb is tender, 40–50 minutes. Stir in the olives and season to taste with salt and pepper.

Meanwhile, in a saucepan over medium heat, bring the remaining 7–8 cups (56–64 fl oz/1.75–2 l) stock to a gentle simmer and maintain over low heat.

In a large, heavy saucepan, heat the remaining ¼ cup oil over medium heat. Add the chopped onion and sauté until softened, about 4 minutes. Add the rice and stir until each grain is well coated with oil and translucent with a white dot in the center, about 3 minutes. Add the remaining 1 cup wine and stir until it is completely absorbed.

Add the simmering stock a ladleful at a time, stirring frequently after each addition. Wait until the stock is almost completely absorbed (but the rice is never dry on top) before adding the next ladleful. Reserve ¼ cup (2 fl oz/60 ml) stock to add at the end.

When the rice is tender to the bite but slightly firm in the center and looks creamy, after about 20 minutes, remove from the heat and stir in the butter and reserved ¼ cup stock. Season to taste with salt and pepper. Transfer to a warmed platter. Make a well in the middle of the risotto, pour in the lamb mixture, removing and discarding the rosemary, and serve at once.

MAKES 6 SERVINGS

THE SCIENCE OF STOCK

Since stock contributes the savory foundation of any risotto, good homemade stock makes a better risotto; see pages 110–11 for recipes. Stock-making technique illustrates an interesting principle of cooking. When ingredients are placed in cold water and put on the heat, all of their flavor is drawn out into the water. That is why when the stock is ready and the meat and vegetables are strained out, they have no flavor. All the flavor has gone into the stock. A contrasting principle comes into play when making soups or stews: vegetables are added to a hot liquid, which locks in their flavor.

GORGONZOLA RISOTTO WITH GRILLED BEEF

Prepare a fire in a charcoal grill, or preheat a broiler (grill). Lightly coat the beef with oil and season to taste with salt and pepper. Grill or broil until the surface is browned and the meat is medium-rare, 4–5 minutes on each side. Set aside and keep warm.

In a saucepan over medium heat, bring the stock to a gentle simmer and maintain over low heat.

In a large, heavy saucepan over medium heat, heat the ¼ cup olive oil. Add the onion and sauté until softened, about 4 minutes. Add the rice and stir until each grain is well coated with oil and translucent with a white dot in the center, about 3 minutes. Add the wine and stir until it is completely absorbed.

Add the parsley and minced tarragon to the stock. Add the simmering stock to the rice mixture a ladleful at a time, stirring frequently after each addition. Wait until the stock is almost completely absorbed (but the rice is never dry on top) before adding the next ladleful. Reserve ¼ cup (2 fl oz/60 ml) stock to add at the end.

When the rice is tender to the bite but slightly firm in the center and looks creamy, after about 20 minutes, remove from the heat and stir in the butter, Gorgonzola, and reserved ¼ cup stock. Season to taste with salt and pepper. Transfer to a warmed platter.

Transfer the grilled beef to a carving board and cut into slices 1 inch (2.5 cm) thick. Arrange the beef slices on top of the risotto, garnish with the toasted walnuts and tarragon sprigs, and serve immediately.

MAKES 6 SERVINGS

TOASTING NUTS

Toasting nuts brings out their flavor and improves their texture. To toast walnuts or hazelnuts (filberts), spread them on a rimmed baking sheet and bake in a preheated 350°F (180°C) oven until golden brown and aromatic, about 10 minutes.

Put the hot nuts in a clean, dry kitchen towel and rub them together vigorously to remove most of their dark, papery skin.

Toast pine nuts and slivered almonds for about 5 minutes. In all cases, remove the nuts from the hot baking sheet right away, so that they do not continue to cook outside of the oven.

1 lb (500 g) beef tenderloin

Salt and freshly ground pepper

7–8 cups (56–64 fl oz/ 1.75–2 l) meat stock (page 110)

¼ cup (2 fl oz/60 ml) extra-virgin olive oil, plus extra for coating

½ cup (2½ oz/75 g) finely chopped yellow onion

3 cups (21 oz/655 g) Arborio or Carnaroli rice

1 cup (8 fl oz/250 ml) dry red wine, at room temperature

1 tablespoon minced fresh flat-leaf (Italian) parsley

1 teaspoon minced fresh tarragon, plus sprigs for garnish

2 tablespoons unsalted butter

½ cup (2½ oz/75 g) crumbled Gorgonzola cheese

½ cup (2 oz/60 g) walnut halves, toasted (*far left*)

RISOTTO WITH BEEF AND BAROLO

7–8 cups (56–64 fl oz/
1.75–2 l) chicken stock
(page 110)

¼ cup (2 fl oz/60 ml)
extra-virgin olive oil

½ cup (2½ oz/75 g) finely
chopped yellow onion

1 cup (2 oz/60 g) sliced
cardoon *(far right)*

1 lb (500 g) boneless beef
sirloin, cut into 1-inch
(2.5-cm) cubes

3 cups (21 oz/655 g)
Arborio or Carnaroli rice

1 cup (8 fl oz/250 ml)
Barolo or other dry red
wine, at room temperature
(see Note)

2 tablespoons unsalted
butter

Salt and freshly ground
pepper

In a saucepan over medium heat, bring the stock to a gentle simmer and maintain over low heat.

In a large, heavy saucepan, heat the oil over medium heat. Add the onion and cardoon and sauté until softened, about 4 minutes. Add the beef and cook until browned on all sides, 3–4 minutes. Using a slotted spoon, transfer the beef mixture to a bowl and set aside.

Add the rice to the same pan and stir until each grain is well coated with oil and translucent with a white dot in the center, about 3 minutes. Add the wine and stir until it is completely absorbed.

Add the simmering stock a ladleful at a time, stirring frequently after each addition. Wait until the stock is almost completely absorbed (but the rice is never dry on top) before adding the next ladleful. Reserve ¼ cup (2 fl oz/60 ml) stock to add at the end.

When the rice is tender to the bite but slightly firm in the center and looks creamy, after about 20 minutes, stir in the beef mixture. Cook, stirring occasionally, to heat through, 1–2 minutes. Remove from the heat and stir in the butter and reserved ¼ cup stock. Season to taste with salt and pepper and serve at once.

Note: Barolo is a fragrant, rich, and full-bodied red wine that comes from the Italian region of Piedmont.

MAKES 6 SERVINGS

CARDOONS

This winter vegetable resembles celery in appearance, with fleshy stalks that taste like a combination of celery and artichoke. It may brown a bit when cut, but the natural color returns when cooked. Italians usually cook cardoons for a long time, but they are also delicious raw or briefly cooked. If unavailable, substitute fresh artichoke hearts (page 31). If you want to use prepared artichoke hearts, choose the bottled ones packed in oil for this recipe. Since they are precooked, you only need to slice them and add them at the end with the butter.

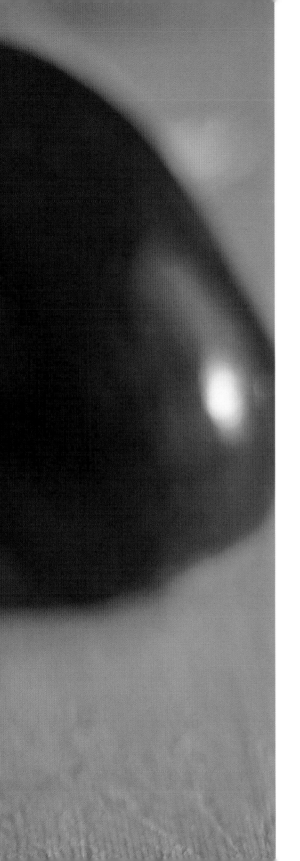

SPECIAL RISOTTO DISHES

The ingenious Italian cook has devised many ways to use leftover rice, some so good that they are worthy of making up a fresh batch of risotto. A risotto rice salad is a refreshing lunch, while risotto shaped into balls or croquettes and fried becomes a delightful appetizer. Tomatoes stuffed with basil-scented risotto or an elegant timbale are perfect sides for a dinner party.

INSALATA DI RISO
78

ARANCINI
81

SUPPLÌ AL TELEFONO
82

RISOTTO-STUFFED TOMATOES
85

RICE TIMBALES
86

SAVORY RICE PANCAKES
89

INSALATA DI RISO

In a large pot of boiling salted water over medium heat, cook the rice, stirring occasionally, until tender to the bite but slightly firm in the center, 15–20 minutes depending on the variety. Add the zucchini and cook for 1 minute. Pour the rice and zucchini into a colander and rinse with cold water until cool. Drain well and transfer to a large bowl.

Stir the olive oil and lemon juice into the rice mixture. Add the tuna, tomato, celery, capers, olives, and basil and season to taste with salt and pepper. Toss to mix.

Arrange the lettuce leaves on a platter. Top with the rice mixture, garnish with the egg quarters, and serve.

MAKES 6 SERVINGS

CANNED TUNA

Seek out imported Italian tuna for this dish. In Italy, the belly meat is used for canning. It is much more tender and flavorful than the solid white albacore more typically used. Choose tuna that is packed in olive oil, which is also much more flavorful than when packed in other oils. Fresh tuna is delicious in this salad as well. Simply grill or sauté a tuna fillet, let cool, and cut into 1-inch (2.5-cm) cubes.

Salt and freshly ground pepper

3 cups (21 oz/655 g) Baldo, Vialone Nano, or Arborio rice

½ cup (2 oz/60 g) diced zucchini (courgette)

⅔ cup (5 fl oz/160 ml) extra-virgin olive oil

¼ cup (2 fl oz/60 ml) fresh lemon juice

1 can (6 oz/185 g) oil-packed tuna, drained and flaked

1 tomato, peeled and diced

½ cup (2½ oz/75 g) diced celery

2 tablespoons salt-cured capers, rinsed and drained

10 Mediterranean black olives, pitted and coarsely chopped

¼ cup (½ oz/15 g) chopped fresh basil

8 large leaves butter (Boston) or Bibb lettuce

4 hard-boiled eggs (page 113), quartered

ARANCINI

¼ cup (2 fl oz/60 ml) extra-virgin olive oil, plus extra for frying

1 small yellow onion, finely chopped

1 celery stalk, finely chopped

1 carrot, finely chopped

½ lb (250 g) ground (minced) veal and/or pork

1 cup (8 fl oz/250 ml) dry Marsala wine

½ cup (2½ oz/75 g) shelled fresh English peas

1 cup (8 fl oz/250 ml) meat stock (page 110)

1 tablespoon tomato paste

2 tablespoons minced fresh flat-leaf (Italian) parsley

Salt and ground pepper

3 cups (21 oz/655 g) Baldo or Arborio rice

6 eggs

¼ cup (1 oz/30 g) freshly grated Parmesan cheese

Pinch of saffron threads, soaked in 2 tablespoons warm water

1 cup (5 oz/155 g) all-purpose (plain) flour

1 cup (4 oz/125 g) fine dried bread crumbs (page 113)

In a large, heavy saucepan over medium heat, heat the ¼ cup olive oil. Add the onion, celery, and carrot and sauté until softened, about 4 minutes. Add the meat, breaking it up, and cook until browned, 4–5 minutes. Add the wine and deglaze the pan, stirring to scrape up the browned bits from the bottom. Cook over high heat to reduce the liquid by half. Add the peas, stock, tomato paste, and parsley, reduce the heat to medium-low, and cook until thickened, 15–20 minutes. Season to taste with salt and pepper.

In a large pot of salted boiling water over medium heat, cook the rice, stirring often, until tender to the bite but slightly firm in the center, 15–20 minutes depending on the variety. Drain and spread on a baking sheet to cool.

In a small bowl, beat 3 of the eggs. Place the cooled rice in another bowl and add the beaten eggs, the cheese, and the saffron mixture. Mix well. Season to taste with salt and pepper.

Place a large spoonful of rice mixture in your palm, pack it lightly, and make an indentation in the center. Place a tablespoonful of the meat mixture in the indentation. Cover the meat with another large spoonful of rice, sealing the meat in the center. Pack firmly into balls about 2 inches (5 cm) in diameter. Set aside.

In a small, deep bowl, beat the remaining 3 eggs. Put the flour and bread crumbs into separate small, deep bowls. Coat each rice ball with flour, then egg, and then crumbs. Set aside.

In a large frying pan, pour oil to a depth of 1 inch (2.5 cm) and heat over medium heat until the oil shimmers. Working in batches, fry the rice balls (page 82), turning frequently, until golden brown, 3–4 minutes. Using a slotted spoon, transfer to paper towels to drain. Keep warm in a low (200°F/95°C) oven while frying the remaining balls. Serve at once.

MAKES ABOUT 24 BALLS, OR 6 SERVINGS

ARANCINI

These fried stuffed rice balls, called *arancini,* or "little oranges," in Italian (due to their shape), are found all over Italy, but are especially favored in the south, where oranges are a major crop. Found in restaurants and street stands alike, *arancini* are delicious either piping hot or at room temperature. At home, they make a satisfying first course. If you like, make them even smaller and pass them on appetizer trays. The best way to work with the sticky rice mixture is to use one hand for holding and shaping the rice, while keeping the other hand somewhat clean for handling the spoon.

SUPPLÌ AL TELEFONO

FRYING SAVVY

In Italian, these little croquettes are called *supplì al telefono,* or "telephone wires," because when broken in half, the melted mozzarella creates a strand between the two pieces. The key to making *supplì* is keeping the oil at the proper temperature. Oil for frying should be heated to 350°–375°F (180°–190°C). If it is not hot enough, it will be absorbed by the food instead of creating a delightfully crisp golden surface. On the other hand, the oil should not be heated above 400°F (200°C), or it may begin to smoke. Novice cooks may want to use a deep-frying thermometer to keep track of the oil temperature.

In a saucepan over medium heat, bring the stock to a simmer and maintain over low heat. In a large, heavy saucepan, heat the ¼ cup olive oil over medium heat. Add the onion and sauté until softened, about 4 minutes. Add the rice and stir until each grain is well coated with oil and translucent with a white dot in the center, about 3 minutes. Add the wine and stir until it is completely absorbed. Add the simmering stock a ladleful at a time, stirring frequently after each addition. Wait until the stock is almost completely absorbed (but the rice is never dry on top) before adding the next ladleful. Reserve ¼ cup (2 fl oz/60 ml) stock to add at the end.

When the rice is tender to the bite but slightly firm in the center, after about 20 minutes, remove from the heat and stir in the butter and reserved ¼ cup stock. Season with salt and pepper. Spread the risotto on a baking sheet and let cool. Transfer to a bowl. Beat 2 of the eggs and stir them and the Parmesan cheese into the rice.

Place a small handful of rice in your palm, pack it lightly, and make an indentation in the center. Tuck 2 cubes of the mozzarella into the indentation. Cover with another spoonful of rice, sealing the cheese in the center. Shape into an oval about 1 inch (2.5 cm) in diameter and 2 inches (5 cm) long, packing firmly. Set aside.

In a small, deep bowl, beat the remaining 2 eggs. Put the flour and bread crumbs into separate, small deep bowls. Coat each oval with flour, then egg, and then crumbs. Set aside.

In a large frying pan, pour oil to a depth of 1 inch (2.5 cm) and heat over medium heat until the oil shimmers. Working in batches, fry the rice ovals *(left),* turning frequently, until golden brown, 3–4 minutes. Using a slotted spoon, transfer to paper towels to drain. Keep warm in a low (200°F/95°C) oven while frying the remaining ovals. Serve at once.

MAKES ABOUT 18 CROQUETTES, OR 6 APPETIZER SERVINGS

5–6 cups (40–48 fl oz/1.25–1.5 l) chicken stock (page 110)

¼ cup (2 fl oz/60 ml) extra-virgin olive oil, plus extra for frying

¼ cup (1 oz/30 g) finely chopped yellow onion

2 cups (14 oz/440 g) Arborio or Carnaroli rice

¾ cup (6 fl oz/180 ml) dry white wine, at room temperature

2 tablespoons unsalted butter

Salt and freshly ground pepper

4 eggs

¼ cup (1 oz/30 g) freshly grated Parmesan cheese

6 oz (185 g) fresh mozzarella cheese, cut into ¼-inch (6-mm) cubes

1 cup (5 oz/155 g) all-purpose (plain) flour

1 cup (4 oz/125 g) fine dried bread crumbs (page 113)

RISOTTO-STUFFED TOMATOES

6 ripe but firm tomatoes, about 8 oz (250 g) each

Salt and freshly ground pepper

1 cup (5 oz/155 g) leftover risotto, such as Basic Risotto (page 10), at room temperature

6 tablespoons minced fresh basil

2 teaspoons minced fresh oregano

¼ cup (2 oz/60 g) tomato paste

2 tablespoons extra-virgin olive oil

¼ cup (1 oz/30 g) fine dried bread crumbs (page 113)

3 tablespoons freshly grated Parmesan cheese

1 clove garlic, minced

1 tablespoon minced fresh flat-leaf (Italian) parsley

Preheat the oven to 300°F (150°C). Lightly oil an 8-inch (20-cm) baking dish.

Cut the top off each tomato. With a small spoon, carefully scoop out the insides, leaving walls thick enough for the tomato to hold its shape. Reserve the pulp. Salt the inside of each tomato and turn them all upside down on a rack to drain for 5 minutes.

In a food processor or blender, purée the tomato pulp until smooth. Transfer to a bowl and add the risotto, basil, oregano, tomato paste, and olive oil. Mix well and season to taste with salt and pepper. Set aside.

In a small bowl, combine the bread crumbs, Parmesan, garlic, and parsley. Set aside.

Fill the tomatoes with the rice mixture, dividing it evenly. Put the tomatoes in the prepared dish. Cover the dish with aluminum foil and bake until the tomatoes are softened, 25–30 minutes. Remove the foil and top the tomatoes with the bread crumb mixture. Turn on the broiler (grill) and place the tomatoes 4 inches (10 cm) from the heat source. Broil (grill) until the tops are golden brown, 2–3 minutes. Serve at once.

MAKES 6 SERVINGS

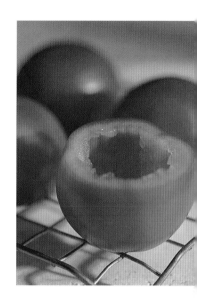

SALTING AND DRAINING

Sprinkling vegetables with salt and letting them sit for a time draws out excess moisture that can interfere with a recipe. After draining, simply brush off excess salt. Do not rinse away the salt, since the vegetable may reabsorb this moisture. This technique is also used in Rice Timbales (page 86) to prevent the eggplant (aubergine) from becoming too soggy.

RICE TIMBALES

Sprinkle the eggplant slices with sea salt on both sides and let drain on a rack for 30 minutes (page 85).

Preheat a broiler (grill). Brush the salt from the eggplant slices and pat dry with paper towels. Lightly coat both sides of each slice with oil. Arrange on a baking sheet and place 4 inches (10 cm) from the heat source. Broil (grill), turning once, until lightly browned and softened (the slices should be pliable enough to line the ramekins), 3–4 minutes on each side. Transfer the slices to a plate and let cool.

Lightly oil eight 1-cup (8–fl oz/250-ml) ramekins. Line each ramekin with the eggplant slices, covering the surface completely and letting the slices hang over the edges. Set aside.

Divide the risotto evenly among the prepared ramekins, then fold the eggplant over the top to enclose. Invert onto individual serving plates, remove the ramekins, and serve.

Serving Tip: The risotto for this recipe can be prepared in advance, making it a perfect dish to keep in mind for entertaining. For a more elegant presentation, garnish each serving with a sprig of fresh herbs.

MAKES 8 SERVINGS

TIMBALE VARIATIONS

A timbale is a molded dish, usually consisting of risotto or custard, made in individual molds or one larger mold. The molds are called *timbales* as well. For risotto timbales, the ramekins may be lined with another food, such as prosciutto slices or grilled zucchini. Or try putting a thin slice of Parmesan or other favorite cheese in the center of the risotto as you are filling each ramekin, then place in the oven at 375°F (190°C) for a few minutes—long enough to melt the cheese, but not long enough to dry out the rest of the dish.

1 large globe eggplant (aubergine), peeled and cut lengthwise into slices ¼ inch (6 mm) thick

Sea salt for sprinkling

Extra-virgin olive oil for coating

6 cups (30 oz/940 g) Risotto with Mushrooms (page 14) or Risotto with Four Cheeses (page 18), cooled to room temperature

SAVORY RICE PANCAKES

3 eggs

3 cups (15 oz/470 g) leftover risotto, such as Basic Risotto (page 10), at room temperature

6 tablespoons (3 oz/90 g) unsalted butter

Freshly grated Parmesan cheese for sprinkling

In a medium bowl, lightly beat the eggs. Add the risotto and stir to blend well.

In a large nonstick frying pan, melt 2 tablespoons of the butter over medium heat. When the foam subsides, drop 1 heaping tablespoon of the risotto mixture into the butter for each pancake, making 4 pancakes in all. Using a spatula, quickly flatten each mound of risotto, then mold the sides to form a thin round 2–3 inches (5–7.5 cm) in diameter. Let cook until the bottoms are browned and the pancakes hold together when you try to lift them with a spatula, 4–5 minutes. Turn and cook until the second sides are nicely browned, about 5 minutes longer.

Transfer the pancakes to a platter and keep warm in a low (200°F/ 95°C) oven. Repeat to cook the remaining pancakes in 2 more batches. Sprinkle with cheese and serve at once.

MAKES 12 SMALL PANCAKES, OR 6 SIDE-DISH SERVINGS

RISOTTO AL SALTO

Traditionally, *risotto al salto,* a thin pancake of cooked risotto, was made with left-over risotto, but it is so good that many people make a fresh batch just to prepare it. If you do so, undercook the risotto by 3–5 minutes and let cool to room temperature. If you are using leftover risotto, bring it to room temperature and remove any large chunks of meat, fish, or vegetables.

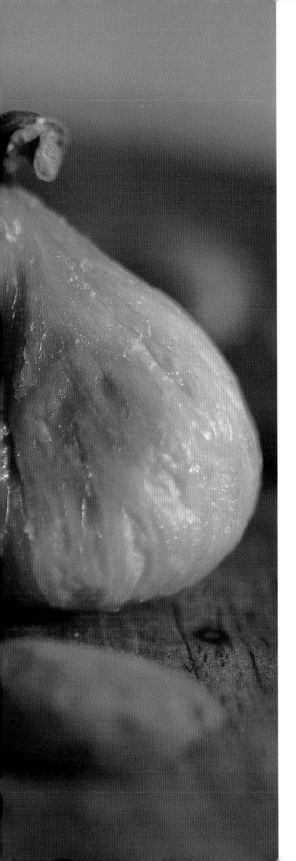

DESSERT RISOTTOS

Pudding is one of the most familiar desserts made with rice, but in Italy you also find rice in cakes, pies, and even ice cream. The gelatinous quality of risotto rice helps hold the fillings together and creates a delicious environment for sweet additions such as mascarpone cheese, chocolate, or figs and other seasonal fruits.

RICE PUDDING TORTE
92

RICE FRITTERS WITH ORANGE SAUCE
95

RICOTTA-RICE TART
96

CREAMY MASCARPONE RICE
99

RISOTTO WITH FIGS AND ALMONDS
100

CHOCOLATE RISOTTO
103

RICE PUDDING TORTE

Preheat the oven to 300°F (150°C). Lightly butter a 9-inch (23-cm) round cake pan or decorative casserole dish.

In a saucepan, combine the milk, rice, sugar, the 3 tablespoons butter, salt, and cinnamon. Cook over low heat, stirring frequently, until the rice is tender to the bite but slightly firm in the center, about 20 minutes. The mixture will still be quite liquidy and puddlelike. Remove from the heat and set aside to let cool.

When the rice mixture is cooled, transfer it to a bowl and add the beaten whole eggs and yolks, the raisins, apricot, rum (if using), and vanilla. Stir to combine. Pour into the prepared pan. Bake until a knife inserted in the center comes out clean, about 30 minutes. Let cool slightly or completely and serve, cut into wedges.

MAKES 4 SERVINGS

4 cups (32 fl oz / 1 l) whole milk

1 cup (7 oz / 220 g) Arborio rice

½ cup (4 oz / 125 g) sugar

3 tablespoons unsalted butter

Pinch of salt

Pinch of ground cinnamon

2 whole eggs and 2 egg yolks, beaten together

2 tablespoons raisins

2 tablespoons chopped dried apricot

2 tablespoons rum (optional)

1 teaspoon vanilla extract (essence)

FRUIT VARIATIONS

This recipe can feature a variety of seasonal fruits and other sweet flavorings. Instead of adding raisins and dried apricots, try fresh cherries. In a small frying pan over medium heat, sauté a small handful of pitted cherries until softened, 2–3 minutes, before stirring into the rice. Or, try quince. Make a simple syrup for stewing the quince by combining equal parts of granulated sugar and water in a saucepan and stirring over low heat until the sugar dissolves. Add a small handful of peeled, diced quince and simmer gently until softened, 20–30 minutes, before adding to the rice.

RICE FRITTERS WITH ORANGE SAUCE

3 cups (24 fl oz/750 ml) whole milk

¾ cup (5 oz/155 g) Arborio rice

⅔ cup (5 oz/150 g) granulated sugar

1 tablespoon grated orange zest

1 teaspoon vanilla extract (essence)

3 eggs, separated

2 tablespoons all-purpose (plain) flour

1 cup (8 fl oz/250 ml) fresh orange juice

1 teaspoon cornstarch (cornflour) dissolved in 1 tablespoon water

2 tablespoons Grand Marnier

Olive oil for frying

2 oranges, thinly sliced

Confectioners' (icing) sugar for dusting

In a saucepan, combine the milk, rice, ⅓ cup (2½ oz/75 g) of the granulated sugar, the orange zest, and vanilla. Cook over low heat, stirring frequently, until the rice is tender, 25–30 minutes. Remove from the heat. Spread the rice on a baking sheet and let cool. Transfer to a bowl and add the egg yolks and flour. Mix well and set aside.

In a small saucepan, whisk together the remaining ⅓ cup granulated sugar and the orange juice. Cook over medium heat, stirring frequently, until the sugar is dissolved, 2–3 minutes. Whisk in the cornstarch mixture and cook until slightly thickened, 1–2 minutes longer. Remove from the heat and add the Grand Marnier. Set aside and keep warm.

In a large bowl, beat the egg whites until soft peaks form. Gently fold the whites into the rice mixture.

In a large frying pan, pour oil to a depth of 1 inch (2.5 cm) and heat over medium heat until the surface shimmers. Working in batches, add heaping tablespoonfuls of the rice mixture to the pan and fry (page 82), turning frequently, until golden brown, 3–4 minutes. Using a slotted spoon, transfer the fritters to paper towels to drain. Keep warm in a low (200°F/95°C) oven while frying the remaining rice mixture.

Arrange the orange slices on a platter and top with the fritters. Using a sieve, dust with confectioners' sugar. Serve at once with the orange sauce on the side.

MAKES ABOUT 20 FRITTERS, OR 4 SERVINGS

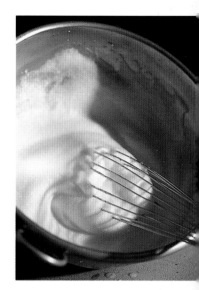

BEATING EGG WHITES

For the best results when beating egg whites, do not let any egg yolk get into the whites as you separate the eggs. Cold eggs are the easiest to separate, as the yolks are less likely to break. Let the separated whites stand at room temperature for up to half an hour to warm slightly before beating. Use a spotlessly clean copper, stainless-steel, or glass bowl; any trace of grease will prevent the whites from whipping up to full volume. Beat vigorously with a whisk to incorporate air. Use at once, since the whites will lose their volume as they stand.

RICOTTA-RICE TART

To make the pastry, combine the flour, zest, and salt in a food processor. With the machine running, drop in 1 piece of butter at a time, processing until evenly distributed. Pulse, gradually adding the water, just until the dough comes together. Do not overprocess, or the dough will be tough. On a lightly floured work surface, form the dough into a ball. Divide in half, then flatten each half into a disk. Place the disks in a zippered plastic bag and refrigerate for at least 1 hour or up to overnight.

Preheat the oven to 350°F (180°C). On a lightly floured work surface, roll out 1 dough disk into a round 11 inches (28 cm) in diameter. Fit the round into a 9-inch (23-cm) tart pan with a removable bottom. Roll the rolling pin across the top of the pan to trim away excess dough. Line with a round of parchment (baking) paper and fill with pie weights or dried beans. Partially bake until firm and slightly colored, about 15 minutes. Remove the weights and parchment paper. Transfer the tart pan to a rack and let the pastry cool. Reduce the oven temperature to 325°F (165°C).

While the pastry is baking, make the filling. In a saucepan, combine the milk and 2 tablespoons of the sugar. Add the rice and cook over medium heat, stirring frequently, until tender to the bite but slightly firm in the center, about 20 minutes. Remove from the heat. Spread the rice on a baking sheet and let cool.

In a bowl, beat the egg yolks with the remaining sugar. Stir in the ricotta, zest, and salt. Transfer the cooled rice to a bowl and add the ricotta mixture. Stir to blend. Pour the filling into the pastry shell. Roll out the remaining dough disk thinly and drape it over the filled tart. Press it against the bottom pastry shell edges in places but do not worry about sealing it completely. Cut 2 or 3 vents in the top and bake until the crust is golden and a knife inserted into one of the vents comes out clean, about 1 hour. Serve warm or let cool to room temperature.

MAKES 8 SERVINGS

FOR THE PASTRY:

1½ cups (7½ oz/235 g) unbleached all-purpose (plain) flour

1 teaspoon grated lemon zest

¼ teaspoon salt

½ cup (4 oz/125 g) cold unsalted butter, cut into tablespoon-sized pieces

4–5 tablespoons (2–3 fl oz/ 60–80 ml) ice water

FOR THE FILLING:

4 cups (32 fl oz/1 l) milk

11 tablespoons (5 oz/ 155 g) sugar

1 cup (7 oz/220 g) Vialone Nano or Arborio rice

3 egg yolks

1¼ cups (10 oz/315 g) whole-milk ricotta cheese

1 teaspoon grated lemon zest

Pinch of salt

CREAMY MASCARPONE RICE

1 cup (7 oz/220 g) Baldo or Arborio rice

2 cups (16 fl oz/500 ml) whole milk

½ vanilla bean, split lengthwise

⅓ cup (3 oz/90 g) sugar

4 egg yolks, lightly beaten

⅔ cup (5 oz/155 g) mascarpone cheese, at room temperature

6 apricots, peeled *(far right),* pitted, and quartered or 3 dried apricots, diced

¼ cup (1 oz/30 g) almonds, toasted and chopped (page 72)

In a large pot of boiling water over medium heat, cook the rice, stirring occasionally, until tender to the bite but slightly firm in the center, 15–20 minutes depending on the variety. Pour the rice into a colander and rinse with cold water until cool. Drain well and transfer to a large bowl. Set aside.

Pour the milk into a saucepan and add the vanilla bean. Place over medium-low heat and cook until bubbles form around the edges of the pan. Remove from the heat.

In a blender, combine the sugar and egg yolks. Process until very thick, about 2 minutes. Remove the vanilla bean from the hot milk. With the motor running, gradually add the hot milk to the blender in a slow stream. Transfer the mixture to a saucepan. Cook over medium heat, stirring constantly, until the mixture thickens and coats the back of a spoon, 6–8 minutes. Do not let it come to a boil. Reduce the heat to low and stir in the rice and mascarpone. Cook until the rice is heated through and the mascarpone has melted, about 3 minutes longer.

Remove from the heat and stir in the apricots. Transfer to a serving dish, sprinkle with the almonds, and serve.

MAKES 4 SERVINGS

PEELING THIN SKINS

The skin of apricots, peaches, plums, and tomatoes will slip off easily if you blanch the fruit. First, score a shallow X in the bottom (blossom) end of the fruit. Plunge the whole fruit into boiling water for 30–60 seconds, depending on the size and ripeness. Transfer to ice water to stop the cooking, then peel away the skin.

RISOTTO WITH FIGS AND ALMONDS

In a saucepan, combine the apple juice and sugar over medium-low heat. Bring to a simmer, stirring until the sugar is dissolved. Maintain at a gentle simmer.

In a large saucepan, melt 3 tablespoons of the butter over medium heat. Add the diced apple and sauté until softened, 3–4 minutes. Using a slotted spoon, remove the apple and set aside. Add the rice and stir until each grain is well coated with oil and translucent with a white dot in the center, about 3 minutes. Add the wine and stir until it is completely absorbed.

Add the apple juice a ladleful at a time, stirring constantly after each addition. Wait until the juice is almost completely absorbed (but the rice is never dry on top) before adding the next ladleful. Reserve ¼ cup (2 fl oz/60 ml) juice to add at the end.

When the rice is tender to the bite but slightly firm in the center, after about 20 minutes, stir in the apple. Cook to heat through, 1–2 minutes. Remove from the heat and stir in the remaining 3 tablespoons butter and reserved ¼ cup juice. Sprinkle with the toasted almonds, garnish with the figs, and serve.

Variation Tip: Other wines that would work well in this dessert risotto are sweet Marsala, Malvasia, or other late-harvest wines.

MAKES 8 SERVINGS

VIN SANTO
This sweet, amber dessert wine has a slightly caramel flavor laced with hints of almond and fig. It is made by drying white wine grapes, usually Malvasia or Trebbiano, and then allowing them to ferment for three or four years in small barrels before bottling. The Italians consider Vin Santo to be a meditative wine, something to sip slowly and with consideration.

7–8 cups (56–64 fl oz/1.75–2 l) apple juice

½ cup (4 oz/125 g) sugar

6 tablespoons (3 oz/90 g) unsalted butter

1 Granny Smith or pippin apple, peeled, cored, and diced

3 cups (21 oz/655 g) Arborio or Carnaroli rice

1 cup (8 fl oz/250 ml) Vin Santo or other sweet wine, at room temperature

¼ cup (1 oz/30 g) slivered almonds, toasted (page 72)

6 figs, quartered lengthwise

CHOCOLATE RISOTTO

3 oz (90 g) bittersweet
chocolate, coarsely
chopped

½ cup (4 fl oz/125 ml)
heavy (double) cream

3 cups (24 fl oz/750 ml)
whole milk

1 cup (7 oz/220 g)
Arborio rice

⅓ cup (3 oz/90 g) sugar

2 tablespoons unsalted
butter

½ cup (2½ oz/75 g)
hazelnuts (filberts), toasted
and skins rubbed off
(page 72), then chopped

In the top pan of a double boiler over simmering water, combine the chocolate and cream and stir until the chocolate is melted. Set aside and keep warm.

In a saucepan, combine the milk, rice, sugar, and butter. Place over low heat and cook, stirring frequently, until the rice is tender, 25–30 minutes.

Remove from the heat and stir in the melted chocolate. Transfer to a serving dish, sprinkle with the hazelnuts, and serve.

MAKES 6 SERVINGS

DOUBLE BOILERS

A double boiler is a specialized set of pans used for gently cooking delicate foods. A top pan, which holds the food, nestles into a bottom pan, which holds simmering water. The water should be maintained at a gentle simmer at all times and should never touch the top pan. If you don't have a double boiler, place a heat-proof bowl over a saucepan. Make sure the fit is snug; steam from the bottom pan should not be allowed to come into contact with chocolate in the top of a double boiler, as this can cause the chocolate to seize, or stiffen.

RISOTTO BASICS

A specialty of northern Italy, risotto has earned a place as a legendary Italian dish. Rich, creamy, and irresistible, it has become a favorite outside its homeland as well. Because risotto can be embellished with any number of savory ingredients, from a wide variety of cheeses, vegetables, meats, and seafood as well as sweet additions such as dried fruit and chocolate, it will quickly become one of the most versatile and well-loved dishes in your cooking repertoire.

ABOUT RISOTTO

Italy's earliest rice farmers were monks, using seeds probably introduced by Arab traders. Monastic histories from the late twelfth century describe large-scale rice cultivation in the region of Piedmont, although the newly introduced grain was initially used nearly exclusively for its medicinal qualities. It was not until the late fifteenth century that rice began to gain acceptance on local dinner tables, prompted in large part by the advent of a food shortage in the face of a growing population. Today, the Padano Plain of northern Italy is the largest rice-producing area in Europe, and new hybrids are regularly selected

for cultivation for their flavor and their nutritional and culinary properties.

Much of the Italian harvest is used for making risotto. Italians have traditionally served it as a *primo,* the first course, after the antipasto and before the *secondo,* the meat or fish course. Nowadays, however, due to its widespread popularity, risotto has assumed additional roles in the meal, appearing as a main course or a complementary side dish as well as a first course. Indeed, a bowl of steaming risotto, a crisp green salad, some country bread, and a good bottle of wine will delight even the most discriminating diner.

Italian cooks never waste anything in the kitchen, so a number of classic recipes for leftover risotto are included in this book, some of them so delicious that you might make a batch of risotto just to prepare one. See Risotto-Stuffed Tomatoes on page 85, Rice Timbales on page 86, or Savory Rice Pancakes on page 89. You can also add leftover risotto to a soup as it simmers. The starch from the risotto adds a creamy texture to the broth, and the grains blend well with other ingredients. Just be careful not to overcook the rice once you add it.

CHOOSING INGREDIENTS

As with all cooking, the key to a successful risotto is in the ingredients. The old adage that the whole is only as good as its individual parts truly applies here. The requirements are simple: high-quality rice, fresh seasonal vegetables, good wine, flavorful stock, and sweet butter. Together they can add up to a mouthwatering dish.

RICE FOR RISOTTO

Good risotto requires a starchy rice. Some rice varieties have more starch than others do, and the Italian rices called for in this book have been selected for their ability to hold their shape during cooking and remain al dente—tender yet firm to the bite—when ready. The method of cooking risotto, adding hot liquid a little at a time as the rice slowly simmers, was developed because an outer layer of protein surrounds the starch. As the stock filters through tiny holes in this layer and cooks the rice, the starch is slowly released, thickening the cooking liquid and giving the dish its characteristic creaminess. Among the numerous varieties of rice for risotto, the four most readily available ones outside

Italy are Arborio, Carnaroli, Vialone Nano, and Baldo.

The Arborio variety is most widely known because it was the first Italian rice exported on a large scale. Excellent for risotto, Arborio rice is recognizable by its large, plump grains with high starch content.

Carnaroli is another rice rich in soluble starch. Because of the consistency of the grains, their high starch content, and their resistance to quick cooking, it is considered the best rice for risotto.

The Vialone Nano grain is shorter and thicker than other risotto rices, with an indentation on the end. It is excellent for risotto because it holds twice its weight in liquid. Vialone Nano Veronese was created from the the crossing of two varieties, Nano and Vialone, and is now popular in the Veneto region.

Baldo, a newer variety, is lower in starch. It is good for dishes like rice pudding, salads, and timbales, but also suitable for risotto.

When deciding which of these rices to use in a dish, consider the amount of starch it produces. In a traditional risotto, plenty of starch is desired, so Arborio or Carnaroli is preferred. The best rice to use for soups or pilafs is a lower-starch rice such as Baldo or Vialone Nano.

Choose a high-quality risotto rice, preferably packaged in canvas bags that allow the grains to breathe. Even though it is no longer on the plant, the grain is still alive. Vacuum-packing and plastic wrap keep out insects, but deprive the grain of air, the rice will not be able to absorb as much flavorful liquid while it cooks. The type of rice and its point of origin should be specified on the packaging. All Italian exports offer expiration dates as well. When you open the package, the rice should have an opaque, uniform color with a smooth surface and no off odor. Old rice, or rice not properly stored, will have a rancid taste. Another sign that the rice is old is if it leaves traces of the starch powder in your hand when you hold it. Store rice in a cool, clean, well-ventilated place.

Do not rinse the rice before cooking; it causes the starch to begin releasing too soon.

OTHER BASIC INGREDIENTS

Unsalted butter is typically used for cooking risotto in northern Italy, as it is the traditional cooking fat of the region. Extra-virgin olive oil is good because it doesn't burn as quickly as butter, and the flavor is also delicious. A combination of butter and extra-virgin oil works well, too. Don't use an inferior oil because in the early stages of cooking, the rice absorbs every flavor with which it comes into contact.

Onion is used in nearly every risotto, but green (spring) onions and leeks are good stand-ins. Other vegetables may be added along with the onion, and the size you cut them will vary depending on the cooking time of each vegetable. Carrots, for example, should be finely minced or grated, as leaving them in large pieces might not allow them enough time to cook sufficiently. Squash, on the other hand, cooks quickly and should be left in larger pieces or cooked, then removed until the rice is nearly done, and then added back in to warm up.

Any wine that you would drink with pleasure can be used in risotto. Its bouquet must be respectable, for its flavor is readily absorbed into the rice. Never use chilled wine; the temporary chill disturbs the steady cooking of the rice, which can result in grains with hard centers.

Since risotto absorbs so much liquid as it cooks, the choice of the cooking liquid is critical. If you are making a risotto that contains meat, use beef or veal stock. A risotto with poultry added is best made with chicken stock, while a seafood risotto begs for fish stock or shellfish stock.

In any case, homemade stock is preferred. Some frozen products are acceptable, but only if the ingredients are natural and there is no added sugar or salt. Most canned broths are often heavily seasoned and usually contain additives that will deter from the flavor of the risotto. Taste both frozen and canned products before using them. In Italy, whole milk is used to cook the rice for sweet dishes, but fruit juice also works well.

Most of the recipes in this book call for stirring in butter at the end of the cooking because it gives the risotto a silky smooth finish. This can be considered optional. When using a top-quality rice with plenty of starch, there is enough creaminess to forgo the butter. Seasoning with salt and pepper should also be done just before serving. Sea salt and freshly ground pepper deliver the most flavor. Cheese is generally stirred in at the last moment. Note that in Italy, cheese is never used in a dish with fish or shellfish, for fear that its strong flavor will overpower these more delicate ones.

RECIPE YIELDS

The final yield of a risotto recipe is about double the uncooked amount of rice, plus any additional ingredients, such as vegetables, meats, and seafood, you have added. In general, 2 cups (14 oz/440 g) uncooked rice serves four people as a main course or six as a side dish or first course, and 3 cups (21 oz/655 g) uncooked rice serves six people as a main course. It is easy to adjust a risotto recipe to serve more or fewer people. Typically, the ratio of rice to liquid (including stock and wine) is 1 to 3.5, and additions may be increased or decreased as desired.

Note that the amount of stock you need may vary, depending on the exact heat level, how much rice is used, and the width of your pan. In addition, some rice varieties absorb more liquid than others do. If you are in danger of running out of stock before your rice is done, add a little water to the pan of simmering stock. Heat it and continue adding as you would undiluted stock. The rice absorbs the most flavor at the beginning of the cooking, so don't dilute the stock until the end, and reserve some undiluted stock for the final addition.

THE RIGHT PAN

Once you have the ingredients for a risotto, consider the utensils you will need for cooking. The equipment is simple: a large pan for the simmering stock, a ladle, a pan for cooking the risotto, and a spoon for stirring. The risotto pan should be wide and heavy-bottomed. A broad surface will disperse the heat more evenly to allow a uniform reduction of the liquid as it cooks. A heavy bottom will help prevent scorching.

MAKING RISOTTO

Have all the ingredients at room temperature or warmed before you start cooking. If the ingredients are cold when you add them to a cooking risotto, it shocks the rice and causes it to stay hard at the core. It also slows down the process and inhibits the release of the essential starch.

The first step to making most risottos is sautéing onion to add flavor. This is the point at which you will cook any additional flavor ingredients, such as meat, poultry, fish, or vegetables. Some excellent seasonal vegetables for risotto include asparagus tips, fresh peas, beans, radicchio, artichoke hearts, zucchini (courgettes), fava (broad) beans, and mushrooms. Classic meat and seafood additions include chicken liver, quail, mussels, clams, shrimp (prawns), cuttlefish or squid, swordfish, crayfish, and lobster. You can avoid overcooking these ingredients by cooking them until they are nearly done, then removing them and setting them aside while the rice cooks. Even after these ingredients are removed from the pan, some of their flavor lingers and is absorbed at once by the rice. For that reason, do not allow the onion or garlic to overbrown and turn bitter, but rather cook just enough to soften and introduce their flavor subtly to the dish.

Next, the rice is added to the pan and stirred for a few minutes, until all the grains are well coated with oil and/or butter and each kernel is translucent with a white dot in the center. Lightly toasting the rice in fat tempers the protein coating and coats the individual grains with the fat, a liquid-resistant substance that will inhibit overly rapid absorption of the cooking liquid. This allows an even release of the starch for a more consistent creaminess in the risotto. Never allow the rice to brown as it absorbs the fat.

A splash of wine is now added and the rice stirred until the liquid is completely absorbed. The wine deglazes the pan, loosening any cooked bits stuck to the bottom and returning them to the cooking mass. Now, gently simmering stock is added a ladleful at a time. As you begin to add the stock, adjust the heat so that the rice cooks briskly but not so quickly that the grains start to fall apart. Keep the grains *bagnato*, bathed in broth, so that they don't dry out, but wait until the stock is nearly fully absorbed before adding the next ladleful. The slow addition of the liquid controls the release of starch; what isn't absorbed evaporates. Keep stirring frequently. The stirring helps the fat and starch join and keeps the rice from scorching.

Adding the stock generally takes about 20 minutes. The cooking time depends on the kind of rice used, how it has been processed, and the desired degree of doneness. The Italians like their risotto al dente—still somewhat firm to the bite. There are differences in the desired consistency, however: more robust risottos have a denser finish, while more delicate dishes such as seafood and vegetable risottos are nicely served with more stock and a juicier finish. In any case, the final risotto should be lightly creamy, and each grain should be fluffy. The best way to determine doneness is to try a few grains. Remember that rice, like pasta, continues to cook from the residual heat even after being placed in a serving dish. It also continues to release starch and absorb the existing liquid. For that reason, add a little more stock, about ¼ cup (2 fl oz/ 60 ml) just before serving.

Most of the recipes in this book call for adding butter and Parmesan cheese to the risotto just before serving. These ingredients add a silky finish. For an even richer risotto, stir in a few tablespoons of heavy (double) cream in addition to the butter.

The finished risotto is sensitive to timing. It should be served at once, not partially cooked and then finished just before serving. Any disruption of the cooking process will cause a flawed end result.

Shown opposite are the basic steps for making risotto.

1 Sautéing the onion: In a wide, heavy saucepan, heat oil and/or butter over medium heat. Add the onion and sauté until softened.

2 Coating the rice: Add the rice to the pan with the onion and stir until the grains are well coated with oil and/or butter and are translucent with a white dot in the center, about 3 minutes. A splash of wine is often added at this point to deglaze the pan.

3 Adding the stock: Add gently simmering stock to the rice, a ladleful at a time, stirring frequently after each addition. Wait until the stock is almost completely absorbed (but the rice is never dry on top) before adding the next ladleful. Reserve about ¼ cup (2 fl oz/ 60 ml) stock to add at the end.

4 Stirring in the final ingredients: When the rice is tender to the bite but slightly firm in the center and looks creamy, after about 20 minutes, add any reserved vegetables or other ingredients called for in a recipe. Cook to heat through, then remove from the heat and add a tablespoon of butter, freshly grated Parmesan cheese, and the reserved ¼ cup stock. Season to taste with salt and pepper and serve at once.

BASIC RECIPES

Even when made with imported Italian rice, the finest butter or olive oil, and good wine, your risotto will disappoint you if your stock is not first-rate. Stock, at its best a rich essence of poultry, meat, fish, shellfish, or vegetables, is absorbed into the rice throughout the cooking, so that the finished dish is infused with its flavor. Homemade stock, of course, is preferred, as only then can you be assured of the stock's quality.

Although making stock, especially long-cooking meat stock, is time consuming, it is not difficult. Once the ingredients, which typically require only simple preparation such as peeling and chopping, are in the pot, the stock simmers with little attention. Taking the time yields the cook an ample quantity, some of which can be used immediately and the balance of which can be refrigerated or frozen for future use.

Here are recipes for five stocks, a well-rounded selection to cover any risotto you decide to make.

CHICKEN STOCK

1 chicken, about 3 lb (1.5 kg), cut up, or 6 lb (3 kg) chicken parts such as backs, wings, and necks

1 carrot, peeled and cut into ½-inch (12-mm) pieces

1 celery stalk, cut into ½-inch (12-mm) pieces

1 yellow onion, cut into ½-inch (12-mm) pieces

1 bouquet garni (page 113)

4 qt (4 l) water

In a stockpot, combine the chicken, carrot, celery, onion, bouquet garni, and water and bring to a boil over high heat. Reduce the heat to low and skim the foam from the top. Simmer, uncovered, for 2 hours, skimming occasionally.

Strain the stock through a sieve into another container and discard the solids. Let cool. Cover and refrigerate until the fat solidifies. Discard the congealed fat. Cover and refrigerate for up to 3 days or freeze for up to 3 months. Makes about 3 qt (3 l).

MEAT STOCK

6 lb (3 kg) beef or veal shank bones, cut into 3-inch (7.5-cm) lengths

2 yellow onions, cut into 1-inch (2.5-cm) pieces

2 carrots, peeled and cut into 1-inch (2.5-cm) pieces

1 celery stalk, cut into 1-inch (2.5-cm) pieces

1 bouquet garni (page 113)

12 qt (12 l) water

Preheat the oven to 425°F (220°C). Put the bones and onions in a lightly oiled roasting pan and roast until well browned, 35–40 minutes.

In a large stockpot, combine the bones, onions, carrots, celery, bouquet garni, and water and bring to a boil over high heat. Reduce the heat to low and skim the foam from the top. Simmer, uncovered, for at least 3 hours or up to 6 hours, skimming occasionally.

Strain the stock through a sieve into another container and discard the solids. Let cool. Cover and refrigerate until the fat solidifies. Discard the congealed fat. Cover and refrigerate for up to 3 days or freeze for up to 3 months. Makes about 5 qt (5 l).

FISH STOCK

¼ cup (2 fl oz/60 ml) extra-virgin olive oil

1 yellow onion, coarsely chopped

1 carrot, peeled and coarsely chopped

2 celery stalks, coarsely chopped

½ cup (4 fl oz/125 ml) dry white wine

4 qt (4 l) water

2 lb (1 kg) fish bones and parts from white-fleshed fish

1 bouquet garni (page 113)

In a large stockpot, heat the olive oil over medium heat. Add the onion, carrot, and celery and sauté until softened but not browned, 4–5 minutes. Add the wine and deglaze the pot, stirring to scrape up the browned bits from the bottom. Raise the heat to medium-high and cook until the wine is almost completely evaporated. Add the water, fish bones and parts, and bouquet garni and bring to a boil. Reduce the heat to low and simmer, uncovered, for 30 minutes, skimming occasionally.

Strain the stock through a sieve into another container and discard the solids. Let cool. Cover and refrigerate for up to 2 days or freeze for up to 2 months. Makes about 3.75 qt (3.75 l).

SHELLFISH STOCK

¼ cup (2 fl oz/60 ml) extra-virgin olive oil

1 yellow onion, coarsely chopped

1 carrot, peeled and coarsely chopped

2 celery stalks, coarsely chopped

½ cup (4 fl oz/125 ml) dry white wine

4 qt (4 l) water

At least 6 cups (6 oz/185 g) shrimp (prawn) shells

1 bouquet garni (page 113)

In a large stockpot, heat the olive oil over medium heat. Add the onion, carrot, and celery and sauté until softened but not browned, 4–5 minutes. Add the wine and deglaze the pot, stirring to scrape up the browned bits from the bottom. Raise the heat to medium-high and cook until the wine is almost completely evaporated. Add the water, shells, and bouquet garni and bring to a boil. Reduce the heat to low and simmer, uncovered, for 30 minutes, skimming occasionally.

Strain the stock through a sieve into another container and discard the solids. Let cool. Cover and refrigerate for up to 2 days or freeze for up to 2 months. Makes about 3.75 qt (3.75 l).

VEGETABLE STOCK

¼ cup (2 fl oz/60 ml) extra-virgin olive oil

1 yellow onion, coarsely chopped

1 carrot, peeled and coarsely chopped

2 celery stalks, coarsely chopped

½ cup (4 fl oz/125 ml) dry white wine

4 qt (4 l) water

1 bouquet garni (page 113)

In a large stockpot, heat the olive oil over medium heat. Add the onion, carrot, and celery and sauté until lightly browned, 5–8 minutes. Add the wine and deglaze the pot, stirring to scrape up the browned bits from the bottom. Raise the heat to medium-high and cook until the wine is almost completely evaporated. Add the water and bouquet garni and bring to a boil. Reduce the heat to low and simmer, uncovered, for 45 minutes.

Strain the stock through a sieve into another container and discard the solids. Let cool. Cover and refrigerate for up to 3 days or freeze for up to 3 months. Makes about 3.5 qt (3.5 l).

GLOSSARY

AL DENTE An Italian phrase that literally means "to the tooth," used to indicate that rice or pasta has been cooked until tender but still firm at the center, thus offering some resistance to the bite.

ARUGULA Also known as rocket, arugula, a favorite green used by Italian cooks, has deeply notched leaves and a pleasantly peppery flavor. Look for leaves with good deep color and no visible wilting. The spicy leaves are used in salads, pastas, and on pizzas just out of the oven, as well as in risottos.

ASIAGO A cow's milk cheese made in the Veneto region of Italy. Two kinds are available: aged Asiago is a hard grating cheese with a slightly sharp taste, while young Asiago is softer, has a gentle but tangy flavor, and melts beautifully. Use the large holes on a box grater-shredder to shred the young, relatively soft Asiago.

BELL PEPPERS, ROASTING Roasting bell peppers gives them a wonderful smoky flavor. Place the whole peppers directly over a high gas flame on your stove top or use an outdoor grill if it's the season. Alternatively, put the peppers on a baking sheet and slide them under a preheated broiler (grill). Turn the peppers frequently until their skin is blackened and blistered all over. Put the peppers in a paper bag, close it, and let them steam for about 15 minutes. When they are

cool enough to handle, peel the peppers by pulling off the blackened skin with your fingers or a sharp knife.

BOUQUET GARNI A bouquet garni is a bundle of herbs added at the start of cooking to flavor a stock or soup. To make a bouquet garni for any of the stock recipes on pages 110–11, place 4 fresh flat-leaf (Italian) parsley sprigs, 1 fresh thyme sprig, 1 bay leaf, and 4 or 5 peppercorns on a square of cheese-cloth (muslin). Bring the corners together and tie securely with kitchen string to form a bundle. Retrieve and discard the bundle at the end of cooking.

BREAD CRUMBS, DRIED To make dried bread crumbs, dry out the bread in a 200°F (95°C) oven for about 1 hour. Break the bread into bite-sized pieces and process in a blender or food processor into fine crumbs. Dried bread crumbs will keep for up to 1 month in the refrigerator.

BUTTER, UNSALTED Many cooks favor unsalted butter for two reasons. First, salt in butter can add to the total amount of salt in a recipe, which can interfere with the taste of the final dish. Second, unsalted butter is likely to be fresher, since salt acts as a preservative and prolongs shelf life. If you cannot find unsalted butter, salted butter will work in most recipes, but taste and adjust other salt in the recipe as needed.

DEGLAZING Using liquid to dislodge and dissolve the browned bits of meat, poultry, or other sautéed or fried food stuck to the pan bottom as a result of cooking. When making risotto, the liquid used for deglazing is usually wine, but citrus juice may also be used. It is added to the pan after the onion has been sautéed and the rice grains have been coated with butter and/or oil. The resulting flavorful liquid is then absorbed by the rice.

EGGS, HARD-BOILED Hard-boiled eggs that have been overcooked have an unattractive greenish tinge and a mealy texture. To avoid such an outcome, cook the eggs by this gentle method: Put the eggs in a saucepan with cold water to cover by 2 inches (5 cm). Bring to a boil over medium heat, then immediately remove from the heat, cover, and let the eggs stand in the water for 20 minutes. Cool under cold running water, then peel.

GORGONZOLA CHEESE A cow's milk blue cheese from northern Italy with a moist, creamy texture and complex flavor. It may be labeled *dolce* or *naturale*, the former a younger and milder version, and the latter aged, stronger tasting, and more aromatic. Dolcelatte, a particular brand of Gorgonzola *dolce*, is very young and milder than other standard Gorgonzola cheeses.

JULIENNING A technique by which vegetables, meat, cheese, or other food is cut into thin matchstick strips. To julienne, use a chef's knife or mandoline to cut the food into pieces the length of the desired julienne. Then cut each piece lengthwise into slices as thick as the desired julienne. Finally, stack the slices and again cut them lengthwise, this time into narrow strips. Many recipes indicate what size the strips should be. For those that don't, the strips are typically 2 inches (5 cm) long and ⅛ inch (3 mm) wide and thick.

MADEIRA A fortified wine from the Portuguese island of the same name, Madeira varies from mellow and nutty-tasting dry types often served as aperitifs to sweet, robust after-dinner beverages. Stored for at least 3 months in a warm room or tank, and then sometimes further aged in wooden casks, the wine gradually develops a distinctive flavor reminiscent of burnt caramel.

MASCARPONE Thick enough to spread when chilled, but sufficiently fluid to pour at room temperature, this Italian cream cheese is noted for its rich flavor and acidic tang. Similar to crème fraîche, it is sold in tubs in well-stocked food stores and Italian delicatessens.

OLIVE OIL "Extra-virgin" is a term applied to the highest grade of olive oil, which is extracted from the fruit without the use of heat or chemicals. It has a clear, greenish hue and a fine, fruity,

sometimes slightly peppery flavor. It is the preferred oil for making risotto because it doesn't burn as quickly as butter and its delicious flavor will come through in the final dish.

ONIONS

Green: Also known as scallions or spring onions, green onions are the immature shoots of the bulb onion, with a narrow white base that has not yet begun to swell and long, flat green leaves. They are mild in flavor and can be enjoyed raw, cooked, or chopped as a garnish.

Red: Also called Bermuda onions or Italian onions, red onions are purplish and sweet.

Shallot: A small member of the onion family that looks like a large clove of garlic covered with papery bronze or reddish skin. Shallots have white flesh lightly streaked with purple and a crisp texture. Their flavor is subtler than that of an onion.

White: This variety is more pungent than the red onion, but milder and less sweet than the yellow. Some white onions are sweeter than others and are perfect for caramelizing (see page 60).

Yellow: The yellow globe onion is the common, all-purpose onion sold in supermarkets. It can be globular, flattened, or slightly elongated and has parchmentlike golden brown skin. Yellow onions are usually too harsh for serving raw, but they become rich and sweet when cooked.

ONIONS, CHOPPING Following is a quick technique for chopping an onion: Slice the stem end off the onion, halve it lengthwise from the stem to root end, then peel it. Put an onion half cut side down on a cutting board. With the knife tip pointed toward the root end, make a series of parallel vertical cuts at right angles to the cutting board. Do not cut all the way through the root end. Turn the knife so that it is parallel with the cutting board and perpendicular to the first series of cuts, and make a series of horizontal cuts in the onion half, again not cutting through the root end. To chop, slice the onion across the first two sets of cuts.

PANCETTA A flavorful, unsmoked Italian bacon, pancetta is made from the same cut, pork belly, as the more common bacon, but it is salt-cured instead of smoked and has a subtler taste. It is rubbed with a mix of spices that may include cinnamon, cloves, or juniper berries, then rolled into a tight cylinder and cured for at least 2 months. Look for good domestic brands at delicatessens and Italian markets.

PARMESAN True Parmesan, known by the trademarked name Parmigiano-Reggiano, is a firm, aged, salty cheese made from cow's milk in the Emilia-Romagna region of northern Italy. Rich and complex in flavor and possessing a pleasant granular texture, this savory cheese is excellent grated and stirred into risotto or sprinkled over pasta.

For freshness, purchase the cheese in wedges and grate or shave it only as needed just before use in a recipe. If true Parmesan is unavailable, cheeses labeled "grana," a generic term for all the fine-grained hard grating cheeses made in the same area, may be substituted.

PIN BONES Fish fillets have a row of small pin bones that protrude slightly through the flesh. The bones run along the fillet from the head end and above where the belly cavity was. Run your fingers over fillets to find the bones, and pull them out with special fish tweezers or clean needle-nosed pliers—or, if they are very soft, as in salmon, with your fingers. If the row of bones is securely fixed in the flesh, use a paring knife to slit the flesh on either side of the row, then pull out the bones and the small amount of attached flesh.

PROSCIUTTO See page 67.

RICE VARIETIES For information on the types of Italian rice used to make risotto, see pages 105–6.

SAFFRON This distinctive seasoning is highly aromatic and tints food a bright yellow. It is the stigma of a small crocus, and it takes thousands of the tiny threads to make just 1 ounce (30 g) of the spice. Buy saffron threads in small quantities and store them in a cool, dark place. Crush the threads only as you need them; powdered saffron loses its flavor more quickly than do the threads.

SAUTÉING Taken from the verb *sauter,* the word "to jump" in French, "sauté" means to cook food quickly in a small amount of fat. When sautéing, the pan should be preheated with the fat before adding the foods so they sear quickly, and there should be plenty of room in the pan so the foods aren't too crowded and simmer in their own juices.

SCALLOP The most common types of this plump saltwater mollusk are the sea scallop and the bay scallop. The former is about 1½ inches (4 cm) in diameter, while the latter is about ½ inch (12 mm) in diameter and generally has a sweeter taste and more tender texture. In either case, rely on a reputable fishmonger with only the freshest specimens, as the shell-fish often languish in a ship's hold for days before they are delivered to market. Select sea scallops that are ivory rather than bright white, the result of soaking the shellfish in a solution to extend their "freshness"; look for pale pink or pale orange bay scallops.

SEA SALT Created by natural evaporation, sea salt is available in coarse or fine grains that are shaped like hollow, flaky pyramids. Due to its shape, it adheres better to foods and dissolves more quickly than table salt. It also has more flavor than table salt, and smaller amounts should be used to season foods. Stores carry sea salt primarily from France, England, and the United States. The most prized is the grayish ivory *fleur de sel* from Brittany.

SHRIMP, DEVEINING Shrimp (prawns) have a dark intestinal vein, visible in all but the smallest specimens, running along their backs. Recipes call for its removal primarily for aesthetic reasons. Specialized shrimp-deveining tools are available, but a paring knife can be used. Make a shallow cut following the curve of the back of the shrimp just down to the vein. Slip the tip of the knife under the vein, lift it, pull the vein away, and rinse the shrimp under cold running water.

STOCK See pages 110–11.

TARRAGON This mildly sweet herb has long, narrow, deep green leaves and a flavor reminiscent of anise. It is an important member of the French herb repertoire, for its addition to chicken, egg, and fish dishes. Use caution when adding tarragon, as its relatively strong flavor can overpower more delicate ingredients.

WINE, COOKING WITH Wine adds an important element of flavor to risotto and is often used to deglaze the pan after the onion has been sautéed. Choose a good-quality wine—one that you would want to drink—and avoid products labeled "cooking wine," which tend to be seasoned inferior products. For risotto, look for dry white wines such as Pinot Grigio or red varietals such as Barolo. Fortified wines such as Madeira or Marsala, or sparkling wines such as Prosecco, can also be used.

INDEX

SIMON & SCHUSTER SOURCE
A Division of Simon & Schuster, Inc.
Rockefeller Center
1230 Avenue of the Americas
New York, NY 10020

WILLIAMS-SONOMA
Founder and Vice-Chairman: Chuck Williams
Book Buyer: Cecilia Prentice

WELDON OWEN INC.
Chief Executive Officer: John Owen
President: Terry Newell
Chief Operating Officer: Larry Partington
Vice President, International Sales: Stuart Laurence
Creative Director: Gaye Allen
Series Editor: Sarah Putman Clegg
Associate Editor: Heather Belt
Art Director: Catherine Jacobes
Production Manager: Chris Hemesath
Shipping and Production Coordinator: Libby Temple

Weldon Owen wishes to thank the following
people for their generous assistance and
support in producing this book: Copy Editor
Carolyn Miller; Consulting Editor Sharon Silva;
Designer Douglas Chalk; Food Stylist George Dolese;
Photographer's Assistant Noriko Akiyama;
Assistant Food Stylist Elisabet der Nederlanden;
Proofreaders Desne Ahlers, Carrie Bradley, and
Linda Bouchard; and Indexer Ken DellaPenta.

Williams-Sonoma Collection *Risotto* was
conceived and produced by Weldon Owen Inc.,
814 Montgomery Street, San Francisco,
California 94133, in collaboration with
Williams-Sonoma, 3250 Van Ness Avenue,
San Francisco, California 94109.

A Weldon Owen Production

For information about special discounts for
bulk purchases, please contact Simon & Schuster
Special Sales: 1-800-456-6798 or
business@simonandschuster.com

Set in Trajan, Utopia, and Vectora.

Color separations by Bright Arts Graphics
Singapore (Pte.) Ltd.
Printed and bound in Singapore by Tien Wah
Press (Pte.) Ltd.

First printed in 2002.

20 19 18 17 16 15 14 13 12 11

Library of Congress Cataloging-in-Publication Data

Johns, Pamela Sheldon.
   Risotto / recipes and text, Pamela Sheldon
Johns ; general editor, Chuck Williams ;
photographs, Noel Barnhurst.
      p. cm. — (Williams-Sonoma collection)
   Includes index.
   1. Cookery (Rice) 2. Risotto. I. Williams, Chuck.
II. Title. III. Williams-Sonoma collection (New
York, N.Y.)

TX809.R5 J65 2002
641.6'318—dc21
                                    2002023018
ISBN 0-7432-2680-1

A NOTE ON WEIGHTS AND MEASURES

All recipes include customary U.S. and metric measurements. Metric conversions are based on
a standard developed for these books and have been rounded off. Actual weights may vary.